LINUX

MIKE McGRATH

In easy steps is an imprint of Computer Step
Southfield Road . Southam
Warwickshire CV47 0FB . United Kingdom
www.ineasysteps.com

Notice of Liability

Every effort has been made to ensure that this book contains accurate and current information. However, Computer Step and the author shall not be liable for any loss or damage suffered by readers as a result of any information contained herein.

Trademarks

All trademarks are acknowledged as belonging to their respective companies.

Acknowledgement

The Tux penguin graphic was created by Larry Ewing.

Printed and bound in the United Kingdom

ISBN 1-84078-275-7

Contents

1	**Introducing Linux**	**7**
What is Linux ?	8
Choosing a Linux distro	10
Evaluating hardware suitability	12
Making space for Linux	14
Preparing to install Linux	16

2	**Installing Linux**	**17**
Starting the installation	18
Configuring the mouse	20
Choosing the right security level	21
Allocating disk space	22
Creating drive partitions	24
Choosing packages to install	26
Setting the root password	28
Creating a user account	29
Setting automatic login	30
Installing the bootloader	31
Summarizing the installation	32

3	**Configuring hardware for Linux**	**33**
The system control center	34
Customizing the boot menu	36
Setting up the sound card	38
Changing screen resolution	40
Installing a local printer	42
Setting up a TV card	44
Installing a scanner	46
Changing hardware settings	48

4	**Exploring the KDE desktop**	**49**
Introducing the KDE taskbar	50
Launching applications	52
Understanding virtual desktops	54
Changing the desktop background	56
Customizing window appearance	58
Installing a desktop theme	60
Changing the screensaver	61
Setting event sounds	62
Getting help	64

5   Surfing the web   65

Connecting to the Internet   66
The Mozilla web browser   68
Setting up email   70
Storing email addresses   72
Joining newsgroups   74
Transferring files   76
Composing web pages   78
Messaging online   80

6   Touring the Linux file structure   81

The Linux directory tree   82
Standard sub-directories   84
Navigating with File Manager   88
Navigating from the command line   90
File system dos and don'ts   92

7   Handling files   93

Creating a new text file   94
Moving files around   96
Deleting files   98
Making shortcuts   100
Changing access permissions   102
Accessing files in Windows   104
Compressing and extracting files   106
Getting better compression   108

8   Working in a Linux office suite   109

Introducing the OpenOffice suite   110
Documents in OpenOffice Writer   111
Exporting documents from OpenOffice   112
Spreadsheets in OpenOffice Calc   114
Presentations in OpenOffice Impress   116
Charts and graphs in OpenOffice Draw   118
Formulas in OpenOffice Math   120

9   Creating graphics   121

Introducing the GIMP   122
Starting a new image   124
Finding the menus   125
Opening selection dialogs   126
Working with layers   128
Selecting areas   130
Using filters   132
Running scripts   134
Writing your own GIMP scripts   136

Playing sound and video　　　137

Synthesizing sounds	138
Playing recorded sounds	140
Listening to music	142
Watching videos	144
Playing and ripping CDs	146
Burning CDs	148

10

Using the Linux shell　　　149

What is the shell ?	150
Understanding run levels	151
Editing with vi	152
Switching between virtual consoles	154
Moving between shell applications	156
Viewing text files	158
Searching for a word	159
Printing from the shell	160

11

Scripting for the shell　　　161

Using shell commands	162
Editing text streams	164
Substituting variables	165
Creating a shell script	166
Branching a script	168
Looping a script	170
Handling input values	172

12

Extending your Linux system　　　173

Installing packages	174
Removing packages	176
Downloading packages	178
Installing downloads	180
Installing other desktops	182
Switching between desktops	184
Linux resources	186

13

Index　　　187

Foreword

This book examines the suitability of the Linux operating system for everyday desktop computing tasks and contrasts some popular Linux applications with their counterparts in the Windows operating system. It begins by describing how to install and configure Linux on your own computer, then it explores a typical Linux graphical user interface (GUI). Examples show how to navigate the file system, both graphically and from a command prompt, so you will quickly become comfortable with the Linux system.

Linux applications are illustrated to accomplish common desktop tasks using word processing, spreadsheets, presentations, graphics manipulation and multi-media. An introduction to the Linux shell, and shell scripts, demonstrate why its power and scripting capabilities are so admired by advanced users.

Examples explain how to install further applications just as easily as with the Add/Remove Programs feature in Windows. These include applications from a CD-ROM, downloads from the Internet, and even other desktop environments.

Who is this book for ?

The adoption of the freely available Linux operating system for desktop computing is spreading rapidly. If you want to see how its desktop functionality compares to Windows, or you want to examine its reliability and security, or you want to explore the possible cost-savings of adopting Linux, or if you are just plain curious to see what all the fuss is about – this book is for you.

Conventions in this book

The text body of this book adopts certain typestyle conventions to readily identify content of special significance.

Directory and file names appear in bold font. For example:

/home
simple.txt

Shell commands, script code and variables appear in bold fixed-width font, like this:

```
ls -a
echo "Hello World"
$USER
```

Placeholders within syntax examples appear in italic fixed-width font. These are not a part of the actual code but merely indicate where content should be inserted. For instance the *text* place-holder in this example should be replaced by actual text:

```
echo "text"
```

Introducing Linux

Welcome to the exciting world of Linux – a free open-source operating system that includes numerous free applications. This chapter describes the evolution of Linux and explains how you can obtain your own copy. It also illustrates how to prepare a computer so that Linux can be installed.

Covers

What is Linux ? | 8

Choosing a Linux distro | 10

Evaluating hardware suitability | 12

Making space for Linux | 14

Preparing to install Linux | 16

Chapter One

What is Linux ?

Linux is a computer operating system that can run on a variety of hardware including the popular Intel system found on most desktop computers. It is a modern derivation of the powerful Unix operating system that was introduced way back in 1969.

In recent years the popularity of Linux has increased dramatically as computer users have discovered its many benefits:

Pronounce the name Linux with a short "i" – so it's "li – nucks" not "lie-nucks".

- Linux is released under the GNU General Public License that ensures it remains free to all users – no-one can charge for this operating system so you will never have to pay for it. It's available for free download on the Internet but you may have to pay a distribution charge if you prefer to order a copy on CD-ROM.

- Access to the source code of Linux is unrestricted and it may be changed. This has allowed thousands of programmers around the world to refine the code in order to improve performance, eliminate bugs and increase security.

Many web servers are said to have have a "LAMP" configuration – an acronym for Linux, Apache, MySQL, PHP.

- Linux is truly a multi-user, multi-tasking operating system that allows multiple users to simultaneously work with multiple applications without experiencing any traffic problems. Many of the world's web servers run on Linux for this very reason.

- Linux is an extremely stable operating system – continuous uptimes of more than a year are not uncommon. It can be upgraded "on the fly" so it only needs a reboot when adding new hardware.

- There are a large number of quality applications available to run on the Linux platform. These are comparable to commercial applications that run on other operating systems but, like Linux, these too are free of charge. For instance, the free OpenOffice suite offers similar functionality to the Microsoft Office suite and can even handle files in the popular **.doc** format.

- With open-source software, an administrator can know exactly what a program can do and the security dangers it presents. An open-source application cannot secretly gather information about the user or send confidential information to third parties. This assured level of security and integrity contrasts starkly against commercial software whose source code is closely guarded.

...cont'd

The term "GNU" is a recursive acronym for GNU's Not Unix.

The evolution of Linux

In 1983 a visionary programmer named Richard Stallman began a movement called the GNU Project. Its philosophy was that software should be free from restrictions against copying or modification in order to make better and efficient programs. This inspired programmers around the world to create programs driven by efficiency rather than by financial incentive.

By 1991 the GNU Project had created a lot of software tools including the GNU C Compiler written by Stallman himself. At that time many of these tools were incorporated into a Unix-compatible operating system, by a 21-year old student at the University of Helsinki. His name was Linus Torvalds and he named the operating system Linux (**LINUs** – uni**X**).

Linux was made available for download on the Internet so other programmers could test and tweak the source code, then return it to Linus Torvalds. After a period of enthusiastic development Linux 1.0 was made available globally under the GNU General Public License which ensured it would remain free.

Programmers were keen to explore Linux and soon found some amazing uses for it. In April 1996, researchers at Los Alamos National Laboratory used Linux to run 68 PCs as a single parallel processing machine to simulate atomic shock waves. At $150,000 this supercomputer cost just 1-tenth the price of a comparable commercial machine. It reached a peak speed of 19 billion calculations per second, making it the 315th most powerful supercomputer in the world. It proved to be robust too – three months later it still didn't have to be rebooted.

Linux continued to grow in popularity as a text-based operating system while Windows became the dominant graphical desktop operating system. Recognizing that most PC users want the point-and-click convenience of a graphical environment, the Linux camp began to develop a system comparable to the Windows desktop.

"Tux" the penguin is the logo of the Linux operating system. It commemorates an incident in which Linus Torvalds, while on vacation in the southern hemisphere, was bitten on the hand by a penguin.

From a handful of enthusiasts in 1991 to millions of users now – Linux has come of age. Today's sleek K Desktop Environment (KDE) and the Gnome environment now offer a user-friendly alternative for Windows users – Linux for the desktop !

Choosing a Linux distro

At the very heart of Linux is a bunch of tried and tested compiled code called the "kernel". The kernel provides the operating system with its core functionality, much like the engine in a car. It takes care of the basics, such as helping other programs access hardware and sharing your computer's processor among various programs.

In addition to the kernel Linux contains a number of system-level programs, such as the services to handle your email, web connection and bootloader. Consider these as a car's transmission, gears and chassis – without these the engine is not much use.

Linux distributions generally also include a large number of user-level programs – the applications for daily use. For instance, web browsers, word processors, text editors, graphics editors, media players, and so on. These are the finishing touches to the car that ensure a great ride – whitewall tires and soft leather upholstery.

All of these components are bundled together in a wide variety of Linux distribution packages, commonly referred to as "distros". Just as all the components of a car are bundled together to make a complete car.

Many other Linux distros can be found at www.linuxiso.org – the ISO (disk images) can be downloaded to create a Linux installation disk.

In the same way that there are many makes and models of cars there are many Linux distros to choose from. The most well known distros are RedHat, Mandrake, SuSE, Debian and Slackware. Each distro has its own installer and unique default configuration according to what the distributor considers to be the best arrangement. The ideal one for you will depend on your own personal preferences and how you want to use Linux. The most popular distributions are described below to help you choose.

RedHat Fedora

One of the most publicized Linux distros. The installation procedure is simple and straightforward but further manual configuration may be required after installation to provide access to other drives, such as the floppy drive or CD drive. The default installation does not provide suitable security for a server – it requires a custom configuration and downloaded upgrades before deployment as a server. The Fedora Linux distro, and upgrades, are available for free download at **http://fedora.redhat.com**.

Mandrake

Generally regarded as the smoothest installation procedure of all Linux distros. Mandrake Linux includes many user programs and automatically configures other drives for ready access. This great distro is like an enhanced version of RedHat Linux – with a better interface and configuration options. It is highly recommended for those new to Linux and can be freely downloaded from **www.mandrakelinux.com**.

Novell SuSE

A fully featured Linux distro from German distributor Software und System Entwicklung (SuSE), acquired by Novell. It has a simple to use installer called YaST which also allows easy configuration of Linux as a desktop or server. It supports even the most obscure hardware. This distro cannot be downloaded but can be ordered as a boxed set of CD-ROMs at **www.suse.com**. The Java Desktop System (JDS) from Sun Microsystems is also based on this distro – see **www.sun.com/software/javadesktopsystem**.

Debian

This distro adheres strongly to the principal of free software so does not bundle any of the commercial applications that other distros may include. It is extremely powerful and its package management features make it easy to upgrade your system. The Debian Linux distro can be freely downloaded at **www.debian.org**.

Slackware

A compact stripped-down version of Linux without any frills. This distro is better suited to those who are experienced in Linux as the reduced features leave it less user-friendly than other distros. The default installation provides adequate security for use as a server. It can be freely downloaded at **www.slackware.com**.

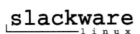

All Linux distributions that are bundled with numerous programs are obviously pretty sizeable. For instance, Mandrake Linux occupies three CD-ROMs. Downloading a distro of this size is time-consuming even with a high speed Internet connection. An alternative is to buy the distro on CD-ROMs from the distributor. Copies made by other Linux users can also be purchased very inexpensively on the Internet from websites such as DistroWatch at **www.distrowatch.com** or try using a search engine.

Evaluating hardware suitability

Before installing Linux on a computer it is necessary to evaluate its hardware specifications for suitability. The table below suggests minimum specifications for processor, memory and hard disk (HD) drive.

Linux can be installed on systems that fall below these suggested levels but performance may be impaired.

Hardware item	Suggested minimum
CPU speed	300Mhz minimum (1.0Ghz + is better)
Memory size	128Mb minimum (256Mb + is better)
HD drive capacity	5Gb minimum (10Gb + is better)

It's easy to discover the CPU and memory information if Windows is already installed on the computer – right-click on the My Computer icon then select Properties to open the System Properties dialog box. The details are displayed under the General tab, as illustrated below.

The CPU and memory details are also usually displayed by the BIOS when the computer gets booted up.

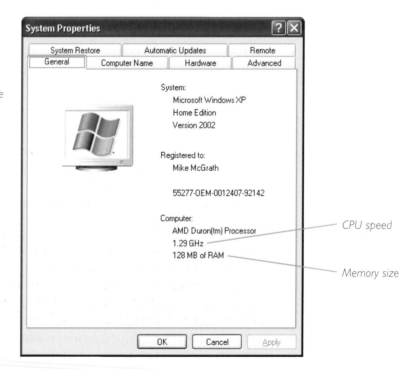

To discover the available HD drive capacity in Windows, click on the My Computer icon then right-click on the HD drive icon and select Properties to open the Local Disk Properties dialog box. Drive capacity information is displayed under the General tab. On the HD drive illustrated below 5Gb of the free space could be given over to Linux.

Devoting 5Gb to Linux on the drive shown here does not leave much space for further work in Windows.

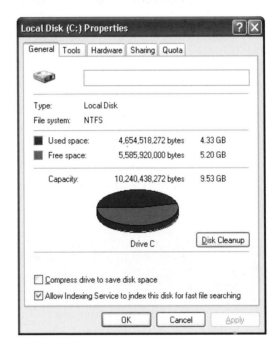

Consideration should also be given to the hardware used to connect to the Internet. Connection via a PCI ethernet card, or on-motherboard ethernet controller, is very well supported in Linux and virtually all hardware of this type is suitable.

If you are really determined to try to get your winmodem working in Linux visit www.linmodems.org to discover lots of helpful advice.

Unfortunately modems are rather more problematic. Many computers are supplied with an internal PCI modem that will only work with Windows software. These so-called "winmodems" are unsuitable for connection to the Internet in Linux. If you have an internal modem and find it is unusable in Linux you will probably have to replace it with different hardware before you can connect to the Internet. Usually the easiest solution is to connect an external modem via a traditional RS232 serial port.

Making space for Linux

An operating system is installed on a defined area of the HD drive called a "partition". When Windows is the only operating system installed on the computer the partition will normally occupy the entire HD drive. In order to install Linux in this situation there are three possible options:

- The first option is to delete the partition where Windows is installed and replace it with Linux partition(s) that occupy the entire drive. This option will delete the Windows operating system along with all the applications and data files that were installed there. It creates a dedicated Linux computer which will immediately start Linux whenever the PC gets switched on.

Resizing partitions is a scary process where data loss can, and does, occur – even in expert hands. All contents of the partition __must__ be backed up before attempting this operation.

- The second option is to reduce the size of the Windows partition, so that it no longer occupies the entire drive, then create Linux partition(s) in the resulting free space. This option should retain the Windows operating system, applications and data files if the Windows partition is not reduced beyond the size they currently occupy. It creates a "dual-boot" computer that allows the user to choose from a menu whether to start Linux or Windows whenever the PC gets switched on.

- The third option is to add a second HD drive to the system. This allows Linux partition(s) to occupy the entire second drive and retains the Windows operating system, applications and data files on the first drive. It too creates a "dual-boot" computer that allows the user to choose from a menu whether to start Linux or Windows whenever the PC gets switched on.

The option to install an additional HD drive for Linux is a popular choice for many people as they have often upgraded their original HD drive to a larger one, and so have their original drive spare. It also has several benefits over the other options:

- The free space on the Windows drive is not reduced

- It removes the threat of data loss through partition resizing

- The familiar Windows operating system is retained

- It distinctly separates the two operating systems

- Drive failure would only disrupt one operating system

Adding a second HD drive

Most modern PCs can accommodate up to four EIDE (Enhanced Integrated Device Electronics) devices, such as HD drives and CD /DVD drives, but typically ship with just two – one HD drive and one CD drive. This means that one or two more drives can be added simply by plugging them into the existing system.

The first HD drive in a system is known as the "master" HD drive and a second HD drive is called the "slave" HD drive.

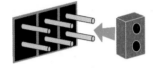

A "jumper" connects two tiny pins to determine if the drive should be regarded as a master (MA) drive or slave (SL) drive. The top of each HD drive usually has a diagram depicting which pins need to be connected in each case.

Before installing a second HD drive first ensure that the jumper on the original drive is set to master and that the wide data cable is connected to the drive by its end plug – not the plug part way along the cable. Now set the jumper on the second drive to slave and connect the data cable using the plug part way along the cable.

If you are not comfortable working inside your PC case a computer shop should be pleased to undertake the fitting of a second drive for a modest fee.

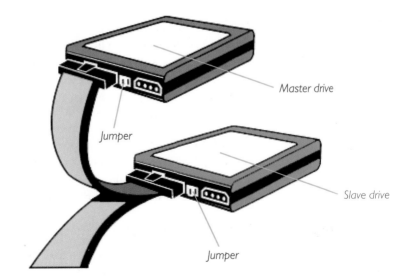

Master drive

Jumper

Slave drive

Jumper

Connect the power cables and start up the PC – both HD drives should now be detected. If the second drive is not detected you will have to change the BIOS settings to auto-seek it when booting.

Preparing to install Linux

If you choose to install Linux on the same HD drive as Windows, it's a good idea to clean up the disk before starting the installation.

This procedure is not required if Linux is to replace Windows on a single HD drive, or if Linux is to be installed on a second HD drive.

In Windows XP, click on the My Computer icon then right-click on the HD drive icon and select Properties to open the Local Disk Properties dialog.

Under the Tools tab click the Check Now button to open the Check Disk dialog. Check both boxes then click the Start button to run ScanDisk – if a further dialog then appears click Yes then reboot to run ScanDisk. The ScanDisk utility checks the condition of the hard disk and takes a while to execute.

When ScanDisk completes click on the Defragment Now button in the Local Disk Properties dialog to tidy up the file system. When the defragmenter finishes rearranging the files on the hard disk you're ready to begin the Linux installation.

Make a backup of everything on your Windows partition before proceeding to install Linux. You probably won't need it, but it ensures that, in the worst scenario, you could recover absolutely all your vital data.

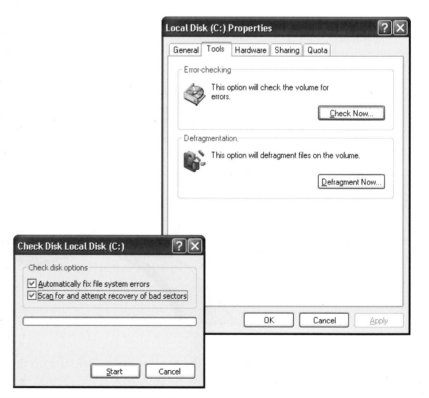

Installing Linux

This chapter walks through the steps of a typical Linux installation procedure using the popular Mandrake Linux distribution. Other distributions broadly follow the same steps but these may appear in a different order and be less intuitive than the highly regarded Mandrake Linux installation process.

Covers

Starting the installation | 18

Configuring the mouse | 20

Choosing the right security level | 21

Allocating disk space | 22

Creating drive partitions | 24

Choosing packages to install | 26

Setting the root password | 28

Creating a user account | 29

Setting automatic login | 30

Installing the bootloader | 31

Summarizing the installation | 32

Chapter Two

Starting the installation

Linux installations begin by booting the computer from the first CD-ROM in the Linux distribution set. This requires the computer BIOS (Basic Input/Output System) settings to seek boot instructions from the CD drive before using those on the HD drive. If your computer looks to boot from the HD drive first (as it normally would) you will need to change the BIOS settings.

On starting the computer a message usually tells you which key to press to enter the BIOS Setup Utility – Delete, F1, F2, Insert, End and Esc are common.

The BIOS Setup Utility can typically be entered by holding down the Delete key right after the memory test when the computer is first switched on. From the BIOS Setup Utility menu choose the option for Advanced features to display the boot device order.

The boot sequence needs to have the CD drive before the HD drive, so it may need to be changed to look like this:

First Boot Device   **CDROM**

Second Boot Device   **HDD-0**

Third Boot Device   **Floppy**

Save the new settings and exit the BIOS Setup Utility. The computer will now reboot and initially look to the CD drive for boot instructions. When the CD drive does not contain boot instructions it uses those on the HD drive as before.

Ensure that the first CD-ROM from your Linux distribution is in the CD drive, then switch on the computer to boot from the CD-ROM. The Linux installer program gets loaded into memory then begins to execute.

The installer program starts out by asking you to select a language. Note that this is not to specify a language for use by Linux after installation but is just to set the language that the installer should use during the installation process.

Click on your preferred language, then click on the Next button to proceed to the next step.

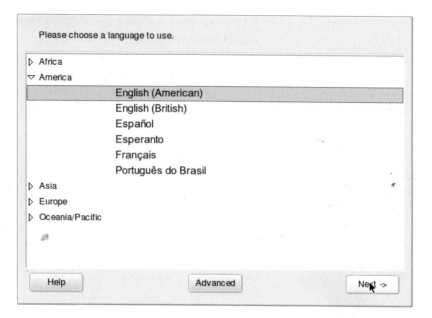

The next step states the License terms and conditions. It is worth reading through this to understand more about the nature of Open Source software. Check the Accept option, then click the Next button to proceed.

Configuring the mouse

The Linux installer provides standard mouse support from the outset but requests you select your mouse type so it can support other types of mouse. If your mouse has a wheel a test is made to confirm that the wheel will be functional in Linux.

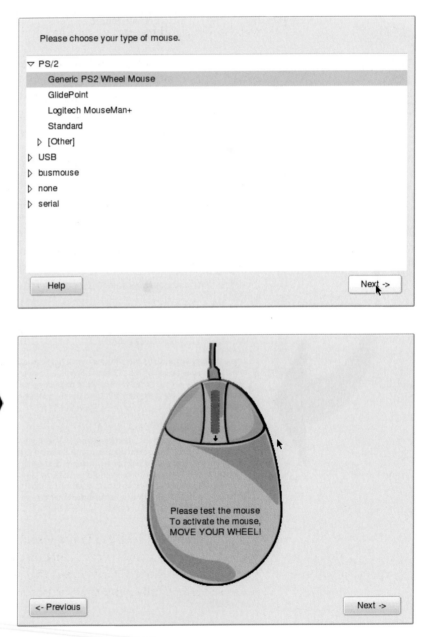

Choosing the right security level

After configuring the mouse the installer asks you to select one of four levels of security, from Standard to Paranoid.

The higher security levels are generally a trade-off at the expense of ease-of-use. Most home users will be satisfied by the Standard default level of security if they only connect to the Internet to use a web browser and to send or receive email.

The examples in this book are all given with the Standard secuirty level selected.

If, on the other hand, you intend to use your Linux system as a server you should really choose a higher level of security to safeguard against possible problems due to multiple connections. This is especially true when the system will hold critical data or is directly connected to the Internet as a web server.

Select the level of security you prefer then click on the Next button to proceed with the installation.

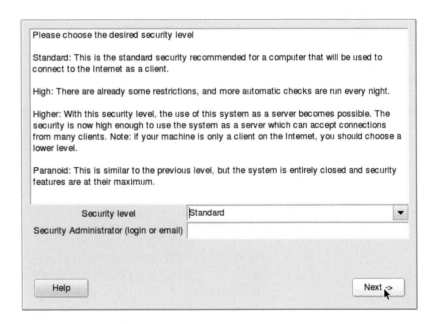

Please choose the desired security level

Standard: This is the standard security recommended for a computer that will be used to connect to the Internet as a client.

High: There are already some restrictions, and more automatic checks are run every night.

Higher: With this security level, the use of this system as a server becomes possible. The security is now high enough to use the system as a server which can accept connections from many clients. Note: if your machine is only a client on the Internet, you should choose a lower level.

Paranoid: This is similar to the previous level, but the system is entirely closed and security features are at their maximum.

Security level: Standard

Security Administrator (login or email):

Help   Next ->

Settings selected during the Linux installation process can be amended later by running the Linux installer again to upgrade the installed Linux system. This means that the security level can be increased later if that should prove necessary.

Allocating disk space

The next step of the installation is to allocate disk space for Linux and will vary according to the configuration of your system.

The installer presents four options in this case:

Take care at this stage not to delete the Windows partition if you want to have a dual boot system.

The first option to "Use existing partitions" may only appear if the system has been previously configured for Linux. For instance, where you want to replace an existing Linux installation.

The second option to "Erase the entire disk" is useful when you want to replace an existing Windows operating system with Linux.

Be aware that the third option to "Use the free space on the Windows partition" may restrict the space available when working in Windows.

Choose "Custom disk partioning" if you need to resize the Windows partition to create space for Linux or if you want to install Linux on a second HD drive. When you click the Next button the installer graphically displays your current partitions. Each HD drive is given its own tabbed window – the master HD drive is labelled "hda" and the slave HD drive, if present, is labelled "hdb".

In the configuration illustrated below two HD drives are present. The master HD drive **hda** allocates its entire disk space of 9.5 Gb to Windows. Clicking on the bar representing the partition brings up options to Delete or Resize that partition

Data loss can occur when resizing a partition so all data should be backed up before attempting this procedure.

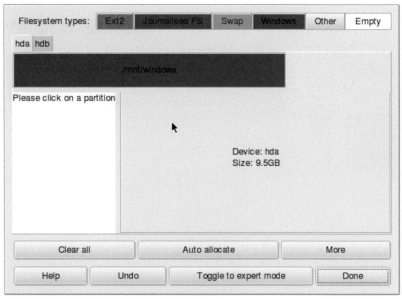

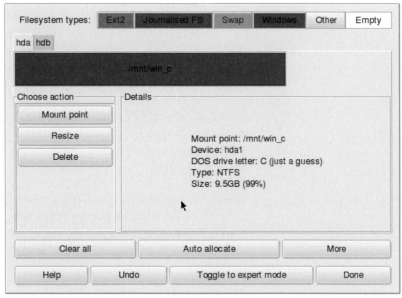

Creating drive partitions

If you are installing Linux on the slave HD drive labelled **hdb** click on that drive's tab to display its partition information. In the illustration below the slave drive is completely empty so it is ready to be partitioned for Linux.

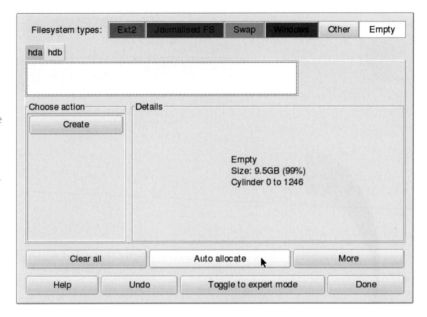

Linux requires that the space allocated to it is split into three distinct partitions - one for the applications and operating system files, one for your own files and a swap area. The easiest way to create these is to use the installer's Auto Allocate feature to split the empty space into three suitably proportioned partitions.

First click on the bar representing the empty area – this could be that of the **hdb** drive illustrated above or the empty area created on the **hda** drive after resizing Windows if you are using a single drive. Then click on the Auto Allocate button to see the partitions appear.

The root partition for the system is labelled **/**, the partition for your own files is labelled **/home** and the swap partition is labelled **swap**. The 9.5Gb empty space shown above gets split into a 5.5Gb **/** root partition, a 3.5Gb **/home** partition and a 500Mb **swap** partition.

Expert Mode allows fine tuning of the partition sizes if desired.

When you are satisfied with the partitions click on the Done button. The partition tables will then be written and the partitions formatted on your HD drive in Linux's **ext3** file system format.

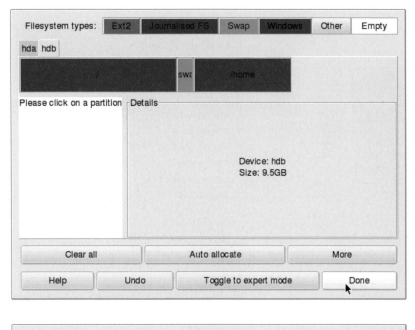

Choosing packages to install

The next stage in the Linux installation allows you to choose what to install from the array of packages on the distribution CD-ROMs. Your choice will depend on how you want to use Linux – the items checked below are popular home-user selections.

As the Linux installer dynamically compiles the list of available packages there can be a lengthy delay before the package options page appears.

Package Group Selection

Workstation		Server
☒ Office Workstation		☐ Web/FTP
☒ Game station		☐ Mail
☒ Multimedia station		☐ Database
☒ Internet station		☐ Firewall/Router
☒ Network Computer (client)		☐ DNS/NIS
☐ Configuration		☐ Network Computer server
☐ Scientific Workstation		
☐ Console Tools		**Graphical Environment**
		☒ KDE Workstation
☐ Development		☐ Gnome Workstation
☐ Documentation		☐ Other Graphical Desktops
☐ LSB		

| Help | Total size: 18 / 3994 MB | ☐ Individual package selection | Next ▷ |

Unlike Windows, Linux ships with a whole range of graphical desktops that can each be customized. The most popular of these are the K Desktop Environment (KDE) and the Gnome desktop environment.

To avoid confusion, until you become familiar with Linux, it is suggested that you only install KDE initially – others can be installed later for further exploration.

Discover more about the KDE project online at www.kde.org

KDE is, arguably, the most popular Linux desktop environment and includes an office suite (KOffice), a web browser (Konqueror), an email client (KMail) and much, much more. It is written and maintained by a world-wide network of software engineers who are committed to free software development. Everyone is welcome to contribute to the development of the KDE project.

Checking each box on this page selects a group of packages to be installed. Experienced users can optionally check the box to allow Individual Package Selection to further refine what to install.

Click on the Next button to install the packages onto your computer. This can take around 30 - 60 minutes, depending upon the number of packages selected and the speed of your system.

Click the Details button to reveal the names of the packages as they are installed.

During installation a slideshow presents various information about your Linux distribution and the installer calculates the duration until completion.

Depending upon which packages you selected for installation the installer may ask you to insert other CD-ROMs from the Linux distribution set. Do so when requested and click on the OK button to proceed.

After the final package has been installed the installer automatically implements Post-Install Configuration of the packages before moving on to the next step.

Setting the root password

Each Linux system has a system administrator account named "root" that has greater access privileges than regular user accounts. For security reasons system configuration can only be implemented by root – regular users cannot make these changes. You should only use the root account for such purposes and normally work in Linux as a regular user.

After installing packages the Linux installer asks you to create a password for the root account.

In a network environment it is essential to create a lengthy alpha-numeric password to ensure that the root account cannot be easily accessed.

The home-user may prefer the option to have No Password to avoid the need to enter a password whenever they want to work as root. This can arise more often than you might now imagine.

If setting a password avoid easily guessed passwords like "admin".

Click No Password to proceed or, if you prefer to have a root password, enter your password in both input fields and then click on the Next button to proceed.

Creating a user account

The next step of the Linux installation requires at least one user account to be created. For the home-user this will normally be the account they will use to logon to Linux for their everyday use.

Enter your actual name in the first field and a short user name in the second field. Now enter a password in both other input fields.

Optionally you can also click on the displayed icon to select a custom icon for this user account.

A user password is mandatory. Make a note of the exact user name and password you enter – you will need these later.

Linux is case-sensitive so take care with uppercase and lowercase characters – user "Mike" will be regarded as a different user to the one named "mike" here.

Click on the Accept User button to create a user account for each person that will use your computer. When all user accounts have been created click on the Next button to proceed.

Setting automatic login

The Linux installer now offers you the chance to select one user account for automatic login whenever Linux is started. For the sole user of a home computer this avoids the tedious procedure of entering a user name and password each time you start up Linux.

This feature should not really be used in an office environment or where the computer has multiple user accounts.

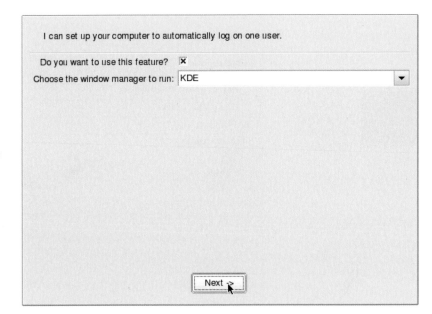

The window manager determines the appearance of the windows – see page 58 on how it can be configured.

The example above elects to automatically login the sole user acccount that has been created. Where multiple user accounts have been created a selection box also appears on this page which allows you to choose the account to automatically login.

If you prefer not to use automatic login the boot process will ask you to enter a user name and password to login to Linux. To launch the graphical desktop type the command **startx** then hit the Return key.

Click on the Next button to proceed to the bootloader installation.

Installing the bootloader

The Linux installer will normally install the bootloader on the main HD drive where it finds Windows boot instructions in the Master Boot Record (MBR) on that drive.

If the installer asks you to choose where to install the bootloader you should select the option to install it in the MBR if you wish to run a dual-boot system. This will present you with an option menu whenever the computer boots allowing you to select which operating system to start – Windows or Linux, etc..

The "Skip" option is useful when running the Linux installer to upgrade an existing Linux installation without replacing the current bootloader.

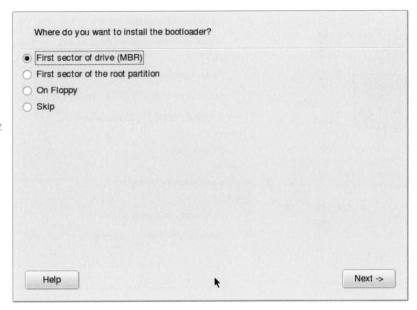

Installing the bootloader onto a floppy disk will allow Linux to be started from the floppy drive when the BIOS setup seeks boot instructions from that drive before the HD drive.

The other options should normally be avoided as they may prevent you from starting Linux on your computer.

Click on the Next button to install the bootloader at the chosen location and the Linux installer presents a summary of the installation.

Summarizing the installation

Each item on the summary page has an associated Configure button to bring up a sub-menu where each device may be configured. This can be done later though and is demonstrated step by step in the next chapter. For now, just click on the Next button to proceed to the end of the installation.

Some of the devices listed here, such as the printer, have only been detected by the Linux installer and must be configured before they will work correctly – see chapter 3.

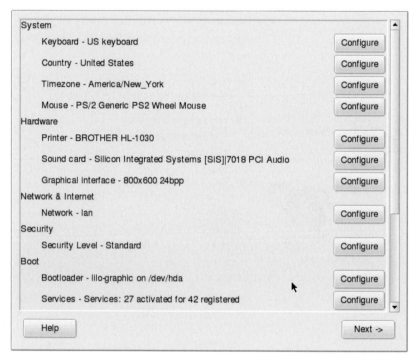

System	
Keyboard - US keyboard	Configure
Country - United States	Configure
Timezone - America/New_York	Configure
Mouse - PS/2 Generic PS2 Wheel Mouse	Configure
Hardware	
Printer - BROTHER HL-1030	Configure
Sound card - Silicon Integrated Systems [SiS]|7018 PCI Audio	Configure
Graphical interface - 800x600 24bpp	Configure
Network & Internet	
Network - lan	Configure
Security	
Security Level - Standard	Configure
Boot	
Bootloader - lilo-graphic on /dev/hda	Configure
Services - Services: 27 activated for 42 registered	Configure
Help	Next ->

Remove the Linux CD-ROM from the CD drive when prompted to do so. Then click the Reboot button to restart the computer. Look out for the bootloader menu when the computer reboots – choose the Linux menu option to run Linux for the first time.

It is interesting to observe the Linux startup process as it lists each service that is being started line by line. Windows' startup follows a somewhat similar procedure but the steps are hidden from view.

Having selected the automatic login feature for a default user the startup process logs that user onto Linux then looks to start the selected graphical desktop. When the KDE desktop has been chosen Linux presents the KDE desktop ready to use.

Configuring hardware for Linux

This chapter demonstrates how to customize a Linux installation for sound and video and illustrates how to add support for printer and scanner peripheral devices.

Covers

The system control center | 34

Customizing the boot menu | 36

Setting up the sound card | 38

Changing screen resolution | 40

Installing a local printer | 42

Setting up a TV card | 44

Installing a scanner | 46

Changing hardware settings | 48

Chapter Three

The system control center

The system control center is the main configuration tool in Linux. In the Mandrake distro the Mandrake Control Center can be found by clicking on the Start button, at the extreme left of the taskbar, then selecting the Configuration menu.

Notice that the desktop icons for the Floppy and CD-ROM state that they are "mounted" – this simply means they are readily accessible. Not all Linux distros automatically mount these drives.

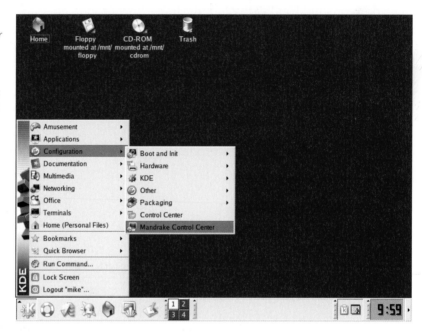

The Mandrake Control Center window has a menu down the left-hand pane. Click on a menu item to reveal associated configuration options in the right-hand pane. For instance, click on the Boot menu item to reveal configuration options regarding how the system boots.

The DrakFloppy tool allows you to create a floppy boot disk if you did not make one during the installation process. DrakBoot enables you to configure how Linux boots up. If you chose the option to have Linux start with a default user automatically logged in, the configuration settings should look like the illustration below.

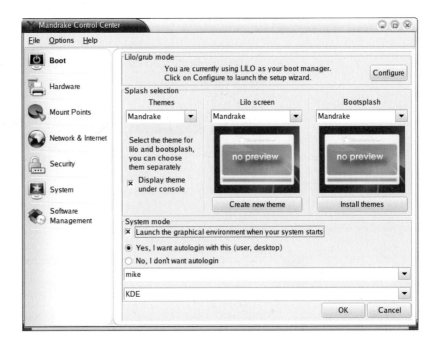

Uncheck the box in the System Mode panel marked "Launch the graphical environment when your system starts" then click the OK button to apply the change. Now click on the Start button on the taskbar then select Logout and reboot the system.

A text-based version of the Mandrake Control Center can be opened by typing mcc or DrakConf at a prompt.

Linux will no longer automatically load the graphical desktop but will open at a login prompt requesting your name and password. Enter these then type **startx** at the prompt, and hit Return, to load the graphical desktop once more. The login details and the **startx** command are the manual steps that Linux completes automatically when you choose the auto-login boot option.

Re-open the Mandrake Control Center and check the box in the System Mode panel marked "Launch the graphical environment when your system starts" then click the OK button to apply the change. Now logout and reboot the system to see that Linux once more starts with the graphical desktop loaded.

Customizing the boot menu

On a dual-boot system the Linux bootloader menu, not unreasonably, makes Linux the default system to start. If you prefer to keep Windows as the default system the bootloader menu can be reconfigured to do so using the system control center.

In Mandrake Linux open the Mandrake Control Center, click on Boot then the DrakBoot icon. Now click the Configure button in the Lilo/Grub mode panel to open the bootloader options dialog.

*The boot device will still be **hda** (first drive) when a second drive has been installed – the boot instructions are installed in the Master Boot Record on the first drive.*

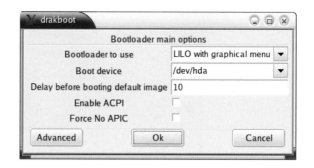

LILO (**LI**nux **LO**ader) and Grub are the bootloaders commonly supplied with Linux. You can choose which one to use in the top drop-down options box. Also the length of time to display the bootloader menu can be set here – it's shown above as 10 seconds. Click on the OK button to reveal the existing boot menu items.

The "linux-nonfb" item starts a version of Linux without frame buffering – it is sometimes needed on systems with old video cards. The "failsafe" item starts Linux in low-level single-user mode – a bit like Safe Mode in Windows.

The asterisk denotes the default system to start on boot. Select any menu item then click the Remove button to delete it or click the Modify button to change how it appears. Only the "linux" and "windows" menu items are essential – the other entries can be deleted by selecting them and clicking the Remove button.

To capitalize the "linux" entry, first select it then click the Modify button. This opens a second dialog box where the label can be edited. Change the first letter to uppercase and uncheck the box marked Default then click the OK button to close this dialog.

Only change the Label and Default settings in the Linux menu dialog – other data indicates some specific locations and should not be changed.

To capitalize the "windows" entry, select it then click the Modify button to open the second dialog box. Change the first letter to uppercase and check the box marked Default to make Windows the default system. Click the OK button to close the dialog box.

The changes to be made to the boot menu are reflected in the boot menu dialog box. Click its OK button to apply these changes.

The default bootloader menu can easily be reinstalled by running the installer on the distro CD-ROM.

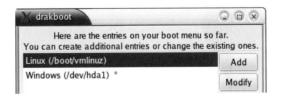

Logout and reboot the computer to see the new boot menu – there should be just the two menu items, correctly capitalized, and Windows should start by default after a 10-second delay.

Setting up the sound card

The system control center can configure drivers for a sound card.

In Mandrake Linux open the Mandrake Control center. Click on the Hardware menu item, then click on the HardDrake icon that appears in the right-hand pane. Select the sound card from the list of detected hardware that appears then click on the Run Config Tool button to open the Sound Configuration dialog box.

Accept the default driver, or choose an alternative from the drop-down menu, then click the OK button to configure the sound card. Although the sound card now has the ability to play sounds a sound server needs to be running in Linux to deliver the sound to the sound card.

Both the KDE desktop and the Gnome desktop have their own control center utilities to configure the desktop environment. These can be used to configure the aRTs (analog realtime synthesizer) sound server to deliver sounds to the sound card.

In KDE, click on Start, Configuration, then Control Center to launch the KDE Control Center. Click on the Sound menu item to expand its menu then select the Sound System entry. Under the aRTs tab in the right-hand pane check the box to "Start aRTs sound server on KDE startup" then click the Apply button.

The system control center is used to configure system-wide settings, whereas desktop control centers are used to configure desktop environment settings – more on desktop control centers in the next chapter.

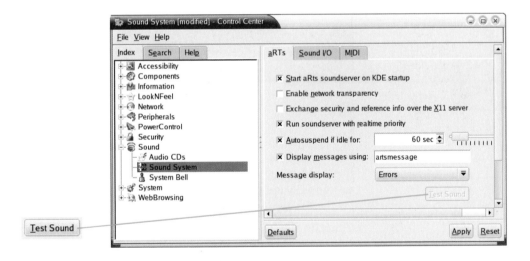

If the test sound does not play ensure that your speakers are correctly connected, then try changing the sound card driver and reboot.

After a second or two the aRTs server gets started and the Test Sound button (that was previously grayed out) becomes usable. Now click the Test Sound button and you should hear a sample sound play.

With this configuration the aRTs sound server is automatically started whenever the KDE desktop starts.

Changing screen resolution

Changing the screen resolution from that chosen during installation can be difficult in some Linux distros – but it's simple in Mandrake Linux, thanks to the Mandrake Control Center.

To Launch the Mandrake Control Center click on Start, Configuration, then Mandrake Control Center. Next click on the Hardware menu item to reveal the hardware icons in the right-hand pane.

Try running Linux at a screen resolution of 1024 x 768 if your setup will support it – some Linux application windows look rather large at lower resolutions.

Click on the icon marked "Change your screen resolution" and the right-hand pane will then display a description of the graphics card and the current settings for screen resolution and color depth.

Click on the drop-down menus and select your preferred resolution and color depth, then click on the OK button.

The configuration changes are not applied immediately – a message in the Mandrake Control Center asks you to "Please relog into Kwin to activate the changes". This means you must either reboot the computer or log out of KDE, then log back in.

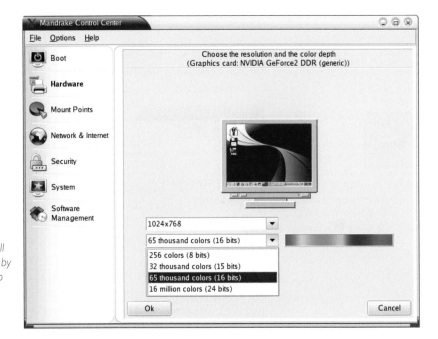

The range of resolutions and color depths will be determined by what your video card can support.

To apply screen resolution changes without fully rebooting the system first click on Start, Logout. Now in the Logout dialog box click the option marked "Login as a different user" then click the OK button.

When the Login dialog box appears simply log back into KDE using the same user name and password – when KDE starts it will appear with the new resolution configuration.

Installing a local printer

The system control center can easily configure a local printer.

In Mandrake Linux launch the Mandrake Control Center and click on the Hardware menu item, then click the PrinterDrake icon.

The Common UNIX Printing System ("CUPS") is a cross-platform printing solution for all UNIX environments. It provides complete printing services to PostScript and raster printers.

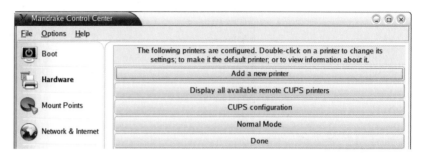

Click the Add A New Printer button then the OK button to auto-detect a local printer – the wizard should then detect the printer connected to the system's parallell port or USB port.

When prompted give the printer a name, or accept the default name of "Printer", then confirm that the printer has been correctly identified so that the appropriate driver can be installed.

GhostScript is an important program for Linux printing. Most printing software under Unix generates PostScript, which is typically a $100 option on a printer. GhostScript, however, is free, and will generate the language of your printer from PostScript.

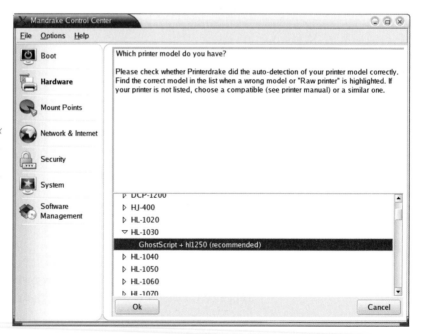

...cont'd

The next step of the printer installation enables default media settings to be selected. Enter preferences for paper size and print resolution then click the OK button to continue.

Increasing the print resolution to a high level can signicantly slow the print speed.

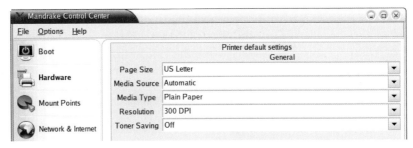

The printer wizard will now ask if you would like to print out a test page to confirm that the printer has been configured correctly. Choose the type of test page you prefer then click the Print button to begin printing. Click the Yes button to acknowledge that the test page print is acceptable. Finally click the Done button to close the wizard – you can now print from application menus by selecting File, then Print.

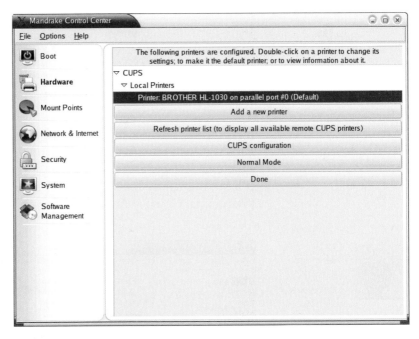

Setting up a TV card

If a TV tuner card is installed in your computer it can be configured using the system control center.

In Mandrake Linux launch the Mandrake Control Center. Click on the Hardware menu item, then click the DrakxTV icon that appears in the right-hand pane. Select the card and tuner type from the lists, or choose "Auto-detect" to let the wizard discover them, then click the OK button to proceed.

The television formats broadcast different numbers of lines at various speeds. If you are unsure of the system used where you are try typing "world television standards" in a web search engine.

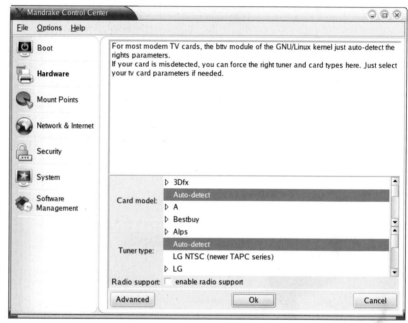

Next choose your location from the drop-down list and select the television standard used to transmit signals in your area – NTSC (**N**ational **T**elevision **S**ystem **C**ommittee) in North America, PAL (**P**hase **A**lternating **L**ine) in the UK and Australia, SECAM (**SE**quential **C**ouleur **A**vec **M**emoire) in France and Russia, etc..

If you're in the USA and receive television via cable choose USA (cable) rather than USA (broadcast).

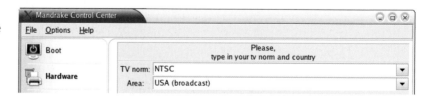

Click on the OK button to proceed and a second window appears in which a range of frequencies are scanned, in turn, to find the TV channels available in your area.

The channels detected will vary according to your location. The ??? frequencies shown here are detected TV channels whose names are unknown – they will still be stored so those channels can be viewed.

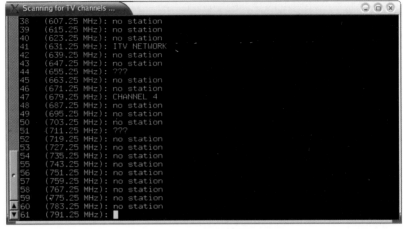

```
Scanning for TV channels ...
38   (607.25 MHz): no station
39   (615.25 MHz): no station
40   (623.25 MHz): no station
41   (631.25 MHz): ITV NETWORK
42   (639.25 MHz): no station
43   (647.25 MHz): no station
44   (655.25 MHz): ???
45   (663.25 MHz): no station
46   (671.25 MHz): no station
47   (679.25 MHz): CHANNEL 4
48   (687.25 MHz): no station
49   (695.25 MHz): no station
50   (703.25 MHz): no station
51   (711.25 MHz): ???
52   (719.25 MHz): no station
53   (727.25 MHz): no station
54   (735.25 MHz): no station
55   (743.25 MHz): no station
56   (751.25 MHz): no station
57   (759.25 MHz): no station
58   (767.25 MHz): no station
59   (775.25 MHz): no station
60   (783.25 MHz): no station
61   (791.25 MHz):
```

When scanning is complete the second window closes and those frequencies that were found to contain a TV channel are stored. Installation of a TV card places an icon on the desktop that can be used to launch the TV application and so view the stored channels.

CHANNEL 4 (mono)

No sound? – Check that there is a lead connecting the Audio Out socket on the TV card to the Line In socket on the sound card.

Installing a scanner

Connecting a scanner to your computer is made simple with the system control center.

In Mandrake Linux launch the Mandrake Control Center then click on the ScannerDrake icon in the right-hand pane. The wizard should then detect the scanner that is connected to your system.

The scanner featured here is the "AS6E" which was mass-produced and sold under a variety of badges. Although popular, it is not generally supported in Linux distros but a driver is available for download from the web at http://as6edriver.sourceforge.net.

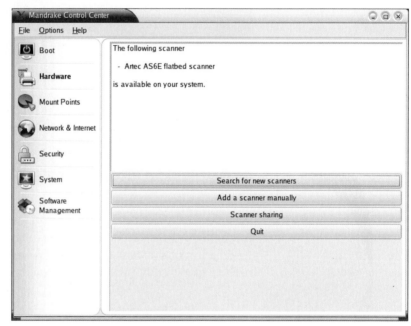

It may then ask you to insert one of the distribution CD-ROMs so it can install appropriate software for the scanner. Typically this will be the XSane program that allows you to import scanned images into your computer.

...cont'd

Scanning images is an art – the balance between resolution and image size is gained by experience.

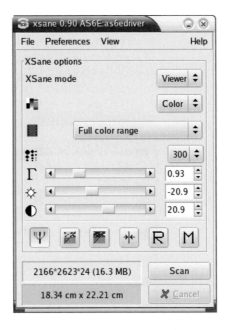

Discover more great titles in the "in easy steps" series at all good book stores or online at www.ineasysteps.com.

Changing hardware settings

The configuration changes described in this chapter are often not as straightforward in other Linux distributions. The user-friendly Mandrake Control Center provides a number of configuration wizards in addition to those already mentioned.

The system control center is used to make system-wide changes irrespective of the desktop environment – settings that apply equally in KDE, Gnome and other desktop environments.

The "Display manager chooser" allows you to select a program for login and session management – these are variations on the original XDM (**X D**isplay **M**anager). The Mandrake Display Manager (MdkKDM) that is installed by default works well enough but you can experiment with others, such as the **G**nome **D**isplay **M**anager (GDM) and the **K**DE **D**isplay **M**anager (KDM).

The "Configure your monitor" and XFdrake wizards are useful to re-configure your hardware when you replace your monitor or video card.

Similarly, you can use KeyboardDrake to change your keyboard layout configuration and MouseDrake if you replace your mouse with a different type.

Exploring the KDE desktop

This chapter examines the K Desktop Environment (KDE) and demonstrates how to launch applications, customize the desktop appearance and add event sounds to enhance the working environment. It also illustrates some useful features which are not found in the Windows desktop environment.

Covers

Introducing the KDE taskbar | 50

Launching applications | 52

Understanding virtual desktops | 54

Changing the desktop background | 56

Customizing window appearance | 58

Installing a desktop theme | 60

Changing the screen saver | 61

Setting event sounds | 62

Getting help | 64

Chapter Four

Introducing the KDE taskbar

When Linux boots into the KDE desktop a splash screen initially displays icons that illuminate in sequence, from left to right, to indicate the progress of launching the environment.

When the sound card has been set up, as described on page 38/39, the sound server gets started upon launch and typically plays a sound when the desktop icon is illuminated.

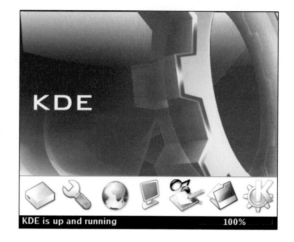

When KDE is 100% loaded the splash screen vanishes and you can begin to explore the desktop environment.

The taskbar, or "panel" in KDE talk, appears across the bottom of the screen by default. It can easily be repositioned to the top or side of the screen – just click'n'drag it to your preferred location.

The Start button is situated, as you might expect, at the extreme left of the taskbar, and features the KDE logo. To the right of the Start button are a number of Quick Launch buttons that are installed by default. Extra Quick Launch buttons can be added by right-clicking on the taskbar and navigating through Panel Menu, Add, Application Button. A menu then allows you to choose for which application to add a Quick Launch button.

Do not choose "Remove Start Applications Menu" – the Start menu will totally disappear if you do !

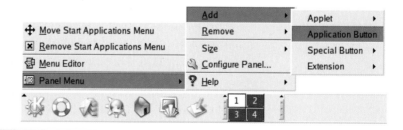

The taskbar is highly customizable and has a special facility for this very purpose. Right-click on the taskbar and choose Configure Panel from the context menu to open the Settings dialog box.

Like most aspects of Linux there are often several ways to do things – the Settings dialog can also be opened from the KDE Control Center with the LookNFeel, Panels menu items.

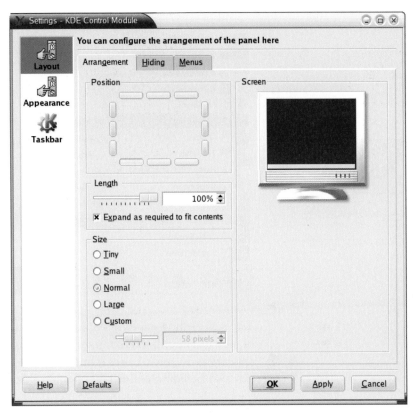

A great Hiding option adds Panel-Hiding Buttons to the ends of the taskbar so it can be hidden by a single click – the animation effect is like retracting a steel tape measure.

The Layout settings allow you to choose the position, height and length of the taskbar under its Arrangement tab. Options under the Hiding tab let you decide when the taskbar should be hidden to reveal more desktop working area. Which applications to include on the Start menu can be edited under the Menus tab.

The Appearance settings configure buttons on the taskbar so they may display tooltips and include individual background images. This makes them clearly appear as buttons rather than just icons.

The Taskbar settings allow you to control how icons of running applications will appear on the taskbar.

Launching applications

Click on the KDE Start button to open the menu. Running the mouse pointer over each menu item displays its sub-menu in a typical fashion – as with the Windows Start menu. Navigate through the menus then click any application to launch it.

Konqueror is both a web browser and a local file manager – it lets you graphically browse through the files on your computer like Windows Explorer, as well as web pages like Internet Explorer.

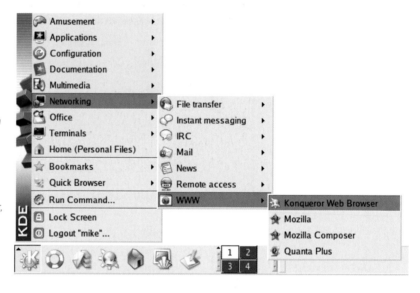

The screenshot above illustrates the Konqueror file/web browser being launched from the graphical menu. Notice that its icon also appears as a Quick Launch button on the taskbar – so Konqueror can also be launched just by clicking that button.

Another way to launch Konqueror is to click the Run Command menu item, then enter the application's name in the dialog box that appears – now click the Run button to open Konqueror.

Konqueror, and other applications, can be launched by typing their name at a command prompt in a "shell" window. This is like running an application from a Command Prompt in Windows.

 Click on Start, Terminals, then Konsole to open a shell window – or click its Quick Launch button on the taskbar. Now type **konqueror** at the prompt and hit Return to open Konqueror.

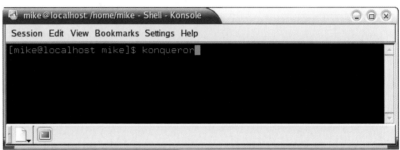

 Konqueror is a windowed application – it can only be launched when the X server is running a graphical desktop environment.

Note that closing the shell window also terminates applications that have been manually launched from it.

Usually it is more convenient to launch an application from the graphical menu, or using a Quick Launch button, but it is occasionally useful to launch them manually from a shell prompt. For instance, if an application fails to launch correctly from the Start Menu try starting it from a shell prompt. This should display an error message explaining why the program cannot launch – resolve this error and the program should then launch correctly.

Understanding virtual desktops

One great feature of Linux desktops not found in Windows is the ability to support multiple "virtual" desktops. This allows you to open applications on different desktops and to easily switch between those running applications.

By default four virtual desktops are available in KDE and these are depicted on the taskbar as a block of four square buttons.

The active desktop in the illustration above is the number one desktop that has a white background. When you open an application on that desktop the window is represented on its taskbar button.

Clicking on a different desktop button presents a fresh empty desktop, but the application continues to run in the original one.

The copy'n'paste process in Linux is simple. Just hold down the left mouse button and drag the cursor over the text to highlight it – this copies the text onto the clipboard. Go to the document where you want to add the copied text and press the center mouse button (or wheel) to paste the text.

Now you can open an application on the empty desktop then switch between the two applications using their taskbar buttons.

In the illustration above a text document is open on desktop #1 in the KEdit application that can be launched from the Applications, Editors menu. A new text document is open in a second instance of KEdit on desktop #2. You can quickly copy'n'paste from the original document to the new document by switching desktops.

The availability of four virtual desktops is usually sufficient for most situations but KDE supports up to sixteen virtual desktops.

To add more virtual desktops first open the KDE Control Center from the Configuration menu. Expand its LookNFeel menu and click on the Multiple Desktops option to open the dialog below.

To move a running application to another desktop right-click on the icon in the top left corner of the window to open the window management menu – then select the desktop to move to, from the To Desktop menu.

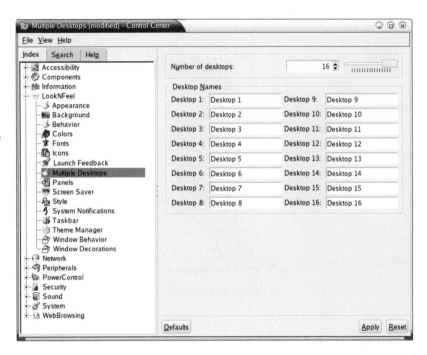

Use the arrowed buttons or click'n'drag the slider to adjust the number of virtual desktops you want. If you wish you may also allocate custom names to each desktop in place of their default names to denote their purpose. For instance, "Text 1", "Text 2", "Graphics 1", "Video", "Browser" and so on. The relevant name appears in the tooltip that is displayed when the mouse cursor rests over their taskbar button.

Finally, click the Apply button to implement the changes.

Changing the desktop background

To customize the appearance of a KDE desktop background first open the KDE Control Center and select the Background option from the LookNFeel menu.

An alternative way to open the Background dialog is to right-click on the desktop and choose Configure Desktop from the context menu that appears – then select the Background option.

In the dialog click the desktop number you want to configure. Uncheck the Common Background checkbox to allow each desktop to have a different background.

Give each virtual desktop a distinct background color to easily distinguish one desktop from another.

Under the Background tab click on the Color 1 color to open the Select Color dialog and choose a color. Repeat for Color 2 to select a second color if desired.

Click on the arrowed button to reveal the drop-down Mode menu and select any of the options. A live preview is displayed in the dialog's monitor graphic to demonstrate how the desktop background will appear in the chosen mode.

Repeat the procedure for each individual desktop. When you're happy with your choice of colors and mode click on the Apply button to set the desktop background colors.

If you prefer to have a graphic image as your desktop background click on the Wallpaper tab in the Background dialog and check the Single Wallpaper radio button.

When the Multiple Wallpapers option is checked the grayed-out Setup Multiple button becomes active. Click this button to open a further dialog box where you can choose a variety of wallpapers that automatically change at any interval you determine.

Click the Browse button to open the Select Wallpaper dialog - this opens in the directory where the default wallpaper files are located.

To colorize a desktop background wallpaper choose the Hue Shift option in the Blending menu under the Advanced tab – drag the Balance slider and watch the preview to see the colorizations. Click the Apply button to colorize the actual desktop.

Check the Automatic Preview checkbox then click on any listed file to display a preview of that wallpaper. When you find a wallpaper that you like click on the OK button to close the Select Wallpaper dialog.

Click on the arrowed Mode button and select an option for how you would like the image to be displayed. Typically this will be the Scaled option to have the image fill the entire desktop background. Now click the Apply button in the Background dialog to set the desktop background wallpaper.

To further enhance a chosen wallpaper click on the Advanced tab and experiment with the Blending menu options.

Customizing window appearance

In KDE there are almost limitless possibilities for the customization of the appearance of windows.

The Color dialog works in the same way as the Advanced Appearance dialog in Windows XP.

On the KDE Control Center LookNFeel menu click on the Colors option to display the color scheme dialog. This contains a clickable area showing the various components of two windows – one in the active state, the other in the inactive state. Click on any component to select it then click on its current color to open the Select Color dialog. Choose a new color, then click the OK button to change its appearance in the preview. Click the Apply button to actually implement the color change in the desktop.

Customized color settings for many, or all, window components can be saved for future use as a Scheme. Alternatively, you can choose one of the standard Scheme options from a menu in the Colors dialog.

The screenshots below show the default window appearance, then how the same window looks after the Storm color scheme has been applied – changing the title bar, border and menu panels colors.

The default KDE window appearance uses KDE Default as the color scheme and Galaxy for both style and window decoration.

Click on the Style option of the LookNFeel menu to customize the appearance of the inner components of a window. In the Style dialog choose any of the predefined styles – a preview of how the components will appear is displayed at the bottom of the dialog. Click the Apply button to implement the Style change.

The screenshot below shows how the window at the bottom of the previous page appears after the System++ style has been applied.

The new style has changed the appearance of the inner panels and the background of the menu buttons.

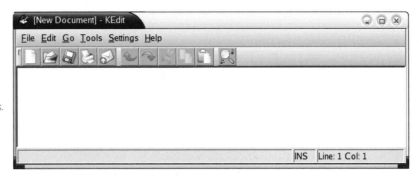

The appearance of the windows' title bar and borders can be customized by selecting the Window Decorations option from the LookNFeel menu. Choose one of the schemes from the menu in the Windows Decoration dialog then click the Apply button to implement the change.

The screenshot below shows how the window above appears after the Keramik window decoration scheme has been applied.

The new window decorations complete the customization of this window – compare its appearance to that of the original on the opposite page.

Installing a desktop theme

Besides the customization possibilities described on the previous pages an alternative way to change the appearance of your desktop windows and background is to adopt a ready-made theme. These change many aspects of the window components to provide a new look with a consistent feel.

Launch the KDE Control Center and select the Theme Manager option under the LookNFeel menu. Several bundled themes are listed under the Installer tab – click on any theme to see a preview of how it will look on the desktop. Click the Apply button to implement the selected theme.

The screenshot below illustrates the Theme Manager dialog with the Wood theme previewed and already applied to the window.

Many Linux themes are available for free download on the web at http://themes.freshmeat.net

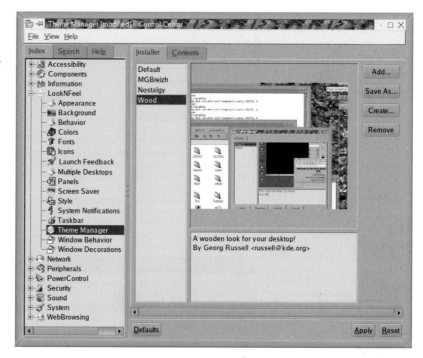

See page 106 for more on handling compressed archive files.

More themes can be downloaded from the Internet – usually these will be in a compressed archive format. Extract the theme file then click the Add button in the Theme Manager dialog and navigate to the theme file to add it to the Installer menu.

Changing the screen saver

Click the Screen Saver option in KDE Control Center's LookNFeel menu to configure a screen saver. A few screen savers are installed by default and more can be freely downloaded from the Internet.

Click any screen saver listed in the Screen Saver dialog to see a preview in the monitor graphic – click the Apply button to use it.

Download screen savers, themes and much more from www.kde-look.org

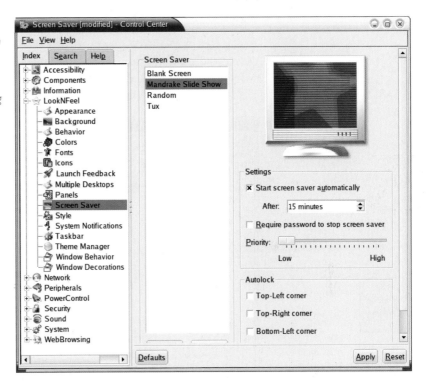

If you want to add a security safeguard to the screen saver check the checkbox marked "Require password to stop screen saver" – then click the Apply button. When the screensaver is running you can only return to the desktop after entering the correct password.

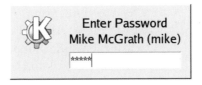

Setting event sounds

KDE can become a more exciting environment when it is configured to play event sounds when you perform various actions. For instance, when an application is launched or closed or when a dialog box appears.

To setup event sounds open the KDE Control Center and select the System Notifications option on the LookNFeel menu. Now click the More Options button in the KDE Window Manager dialog in the right-hand pane.

In the Quick Controls panel at the bottom of the dialog check the checkbox marked "Apply To All Applications", then click Turn On All Sounds and click the Apply button to implement the changes.

Right-click on the icon in the window title bar and select Shade to roll the window up or down – a neat way of saving space on a crowded desktop.

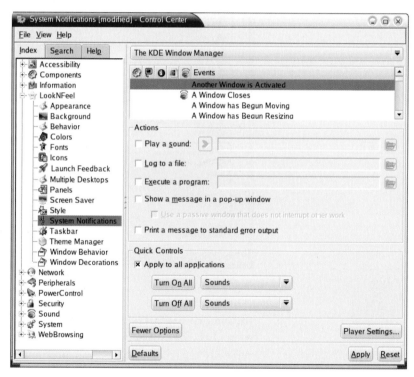

Open an application, such as the KEdit text editor under the Applications, Editors menu, and you should hear event sounds play when the window opens and closes, or is minimized and maximized, or is shaded up and down.

All event sounds can be silenced by clicking Turn Off All Sounds, then the Apply button in the dialog. Alternatively, individual event sounds can be turned off or the event made to play a different sound. With all sounds on, click on the Fewer Options button.

There are other customizing options in the LookNFeel menu – Icons lets you change the icon set and Fonts lets you choose which font to use on the desktop, taskbar and in window applications.

Explore each of the LookNFeel menu options and try changing some of the settings – just push the Defaults button in each dialog box to return to the original configuration.

The list of events displays icons against those events which play a sound. Click on any listed event with an icon to reveal the name of its sound file in the text field below the list.

The arrowed button to the left of this field will play the file when it is clicked. The browse button to the right of this field can be used to assign a different sound file to the event.

To silence the sound associated with this event uncheck the checkbox marked "Play A Sound". In the screenshot above the sound that played when A Window Loses Maximization has been silenced and the field displaying the file name becomes grayed out.

Getting help

Help on any graphical KDE application can be sought in the KDE Help Center. This is launched by clicking the life-belt icon on the taskbar, or on the Documentation menu. Click on the Application Manuals option in the left-hand pane to expand a representation of the applications, as they appear under the Start menu. Navigate to the application you want, then click to open its Handbook.

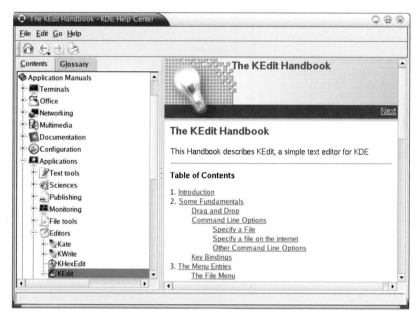

The KDE Help Center can also be opened inside the Konqueror application by typing **help:/** *in the location field. It can also display manual pages by typing* **man:/** *and Info pages with* **info:/** *.*

The KDE Help Center menu also contains an option to view the UNIX manual pages which describe in detail each UNIX command and their range of optional switches. These can also be viewed in text mode by typing **man** at a command prompt, followed by a space and the command you want help with. For instance, type **man ls** to see the UNIX manual page for the **ls** command – this reveals the directory contents.

For help with a command at a prompt type the command name, followed by a space, then **--help** *.*

Some UNIX manual pages can seem confusing but the KDE Help Center can also browse Info pages that provide similar information in a more user-friendly manner. Like the manual pages these too can be viewed in text mode by typing **info** at a command prompt, followed by a space and the command you want help with. For instance, type **info ls** to see the Info page for the **ls** command.

Surfing the web

This chapter illustrates how to perform a wide range of online activities in Linux – once connected to the Internet it's easy to view websites, send and receive email, and transfer files around the world. It also describes how to build your own web pages using free applications that are bundled with most distros.

Covers

Connecting to the Internet | 66

The Mozilla web browser | 68

Setting up email | 70

Storing email addresses | 72

Joining newsgroups | 74

Transferring files | 76

Composing web pages | 78

Messaging online | 80

Chapter Five

Connecting to the Internet

The simplest way to set up Internet access is via an ethernet connection. This will have been automatically configured during the Linux installation process if the Network Interface Card (NIC) was installed and connected.

Modem support in Linux is limited – refer back to the comment at the bottom of page 13 on hardware suitability.

If you are using a dial-up service with a modem, or if you are subsequently installing an ethernet NIC, use the Internet Configuration wizard to configure the connection.

For instance, launch the Mandrake Control Center and click the Network & Internet menu option, then click DrakConnect. The dialog should show details of the NIC and its driver. Alternatively the modem details should appear if you are configuring a modem.

If the detected connection device does not have driver support click on the Hardware menu option. Then select the device from the list that appears in the dialog and click on the Run Config Tool to configure the driver. Return to the Network & Internet dialog and start the Connection wizard.

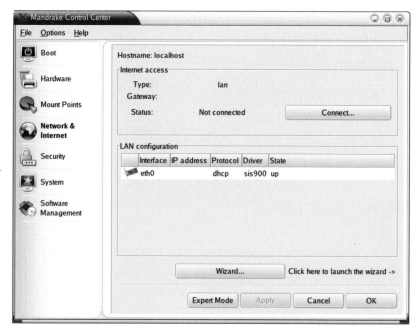

Click the Wizard button to begin Internet configuration. In the first dialog box check the box marked Use Auto-Detection, then click the Next button. The wizard will then search for your connection device and report what it finds in the next dialog. Choose the connection you want to configure, then click the Next button. Check the box to use an Automatic IP address, or manually enter the address details if you want to use a static IP address.

If the wizard asks you to enter a host name or use the default, just click the Next button to accept the default host name.

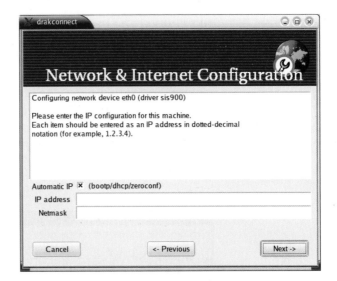

Click the Next button to complete the configuration wizard – the Hostname and IP address details should now appear in the DrakConnect dialog, and the status should have changed to Connected. Launch any web browser and in the URL field type the address **www.google.com** – the search engine page should appear.

Internet configuration in Linux is usually straightforward – you may need to obtain advice from your ISP if you encounter any connection difficulties.

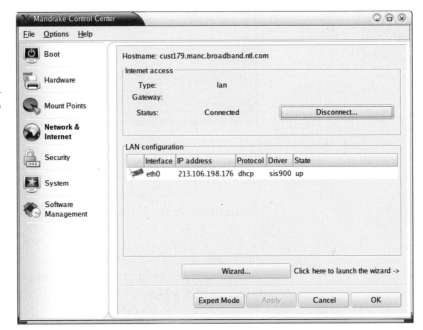

The Mozilla web browser

Most web browsers are based upon the Mosaic browser of the early 1990s – the name Mozilla is derived from "MOsaic" and "godZILLA".

In addition to KDE's Konqueror web browser most Linux distros include the open-source Mozilla web browser. This popular free browser is available for various platforms and contains many powerful features. It has been developed by the open source community from original Netscape browser source code into a very competent, standards-compliant product.

In Mandrake Linux click Start, Networking, WWW, Mozilla to launch the web browser. Type a URL into the location field then hit Return to open that web page in the browser window.

This screenshot depicts Mozilla with the Modern theme applied.

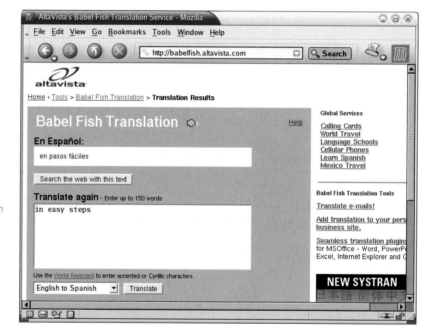

If you're used to Internet Explorer then you will feel instantly at home with Mozilla – but it also has some great extra features. Type a word or phrase into the location field then click the Search button to have the Google search engine return a list of relevant URLs.

Mozilla's appearance can be easily customized – click on the View menu, then select Apply Themes. You can choose from Classic and Modern themes, or select Get More Themes to download other themes from the Internet.

Click on the Edit menu and select Preferences to open the Preferences dialog. The Category menu allows you to configure the browser to your personal taste. The Popup Windows option on the Privacy & Security menu is especially welcome as it allows you to suppress annoying popup windows. Check the Suppress Popups radio button and the Play A Sound checkbox, then click the Select button to choose an appropriate sound file. Click the OK button to apply the change. Popup windows are no longer allowed and a satisfying sound is emanated each time one is rejected.

Linux browser plugins for Java, QuickTime, Flash, Adobe Reader, and Real Player can be found online at http://home.netscape.com/plugins/

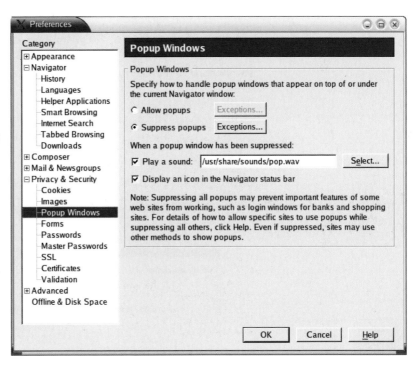

Click on the Tools menu to see the collection of managers that let you have control over forms, cookies, images, passwords and downloads.

Mozilla includes a script development tool called the JavaScript Console – it's found under the Web development menu. Launch the JavaScript Console and type **alert(new Date())** exactly as here into the input field. Click the Evaluate button and a dialog box should pop up with current day, data and time information.

Setting up email

Mozilla includes an email client application called Messenger. This can typically be found under the Start, Networking, Mail menu – or it can be launched by selecting the Mail & Newsgroups option under Mozilla's Window menu, or from the components bar.

On initial launch, the Account Wizard dialog pops up asking you to create a new account. Check the radio button labeled Email Account, then click the Next button to continue. Now enter your own name and email address then click the Next button again.

In the ensuing dialog enter the exact name of both incoming and outgoing mail servers – your ISP will provide this information. In the next dialog enter the email name assigned to you by your ISP. For instance, "mike" for the address **mike@example.com**. Click the Next button to continue.

Now enter a name of your choice for the account. For example "Mikes Mail". It's particularly useful to be able to quickly identify each account when the computer is used by many people.

Click on the Next button to reveal a summary of all the account information. Review the details to ensure they are correct, then click the Finish button to complete the Account configuration.

Messenger includes filters that can mark emails which it suspects to be spam – you can find the Junk Mail controls on the Tools menu.

The Mozilla Messenger window contains a Local Folders directory, where unsent mail can be stored, and your personal account directory. Click the Get Msgs button on the toolbar to retrieve your incoming messages from your ISP.

The right-hand pane contains clickable links to perform various actions in Messenger. To create a new message either click the Compose button on the toolbar or click the Compose A New Message link – they both open a new message window.

The Account folders, such as Inbox, work like those in Outlook so Windows users should be right at home here.

The first time you attempt to connect to your ISP for email a dialog will appear asking you to enter the password for that email account. Enter the password agreed with your ISP. Be sure to check the box labeled "Use Password Manager to remember this password" so you won't need to manually enter the password every time you want to access your email. Click OK to get your email.

Storing email addresses

The Mozilla Address Book allows you to store the email addresses and personal details of each of your contacts on individual "cards".

An email address can be added to a new card from the Inbox folder by right-clicking on the sender's address and choosing Add To Address Book from the context menu that appears.

You can configure Mozilla to automatically add email addresses of outgoing messages to the Address Book. First select the Preferences option on the Edit menu then expand the Mail & Newsgroups menu. Click on the Addressing category and check the box in the Email Address Collection panel. Click the OK button to apply the change.

The Address Book can be opened by clicking the Address Book button on the Mozilla component bar, or by selecting the Address Book option from the Window menu, or typically by navigating through Start, Networking, Mail, Mozilla Address Book.

In the left-hand pane (headed Address Books) click on the Personal Address Book option to see a list of all cards for your email account appear in the top right-hand pane. Click any card in the list to reveal the stored details in the bottom right-hand pane.

To remove a card select it on the list then click the Delete button on the toolbar.

Double-click any card in the list to open the Card dialog where details on that card can be added or modified. Alternatively click the properties button on the tool bar to open the Card dialog for the currently selected card.

New cards can be created manually by clicking the New Card button on the tool bar and lists created with the New List button.

Click the Get Map button to open a local map based on the details stored in the City, State and Zip Code fields in the card's Address tab – in this example it's a map of the New York city area.

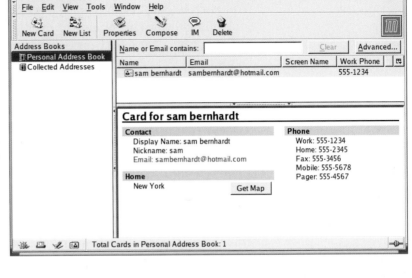

Only set the preferred mail format to HTML if you are sure the recipient allows for HTML – some prefer to restrict messages to Plain Text format.

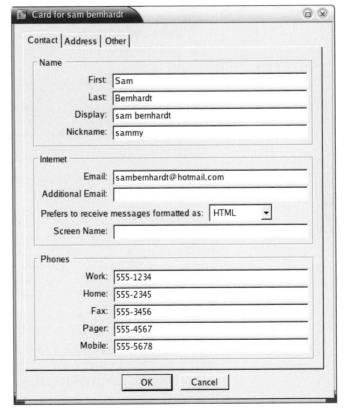

Joining newsgroups

Newsgroups provide online areas for discussion of specific topics. You can join one, or more, newsgroups on topics that interest you and follow the discussion posted by other members of that group – also you may contribute your own views by posting to the newsgroup, but this is not essential.

To join a newsgroup you must first establish a newsgroup account, in much the same way that an email account must be setup before you can send/receive email.

Mozilla News can also be launched from the Start menu – navigate through Start, Networking, News.

In the Mozilla Inbox click on the File, New, Account menu options to open the Account Wizard. Check the radio button marked Newsgroup Account then click the Next button. Enter your name and email address then the name of the Newsgroup server – your ISP will provide this information. Type a name for this newsgroup account then click the Next button to display a final summary of the account information.

Newsgroups may contain uncensored material.

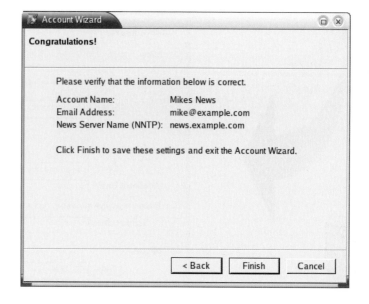

Click the finish button to create the newsgroup account and see it appear in the left-hand pane of the Messenger window. Right-click on this item then choose Subscribe from the context menu. A list of all available newsgroups gets downloaded. Then they are displayed in the Subscribe dialog – select those you wish to join.

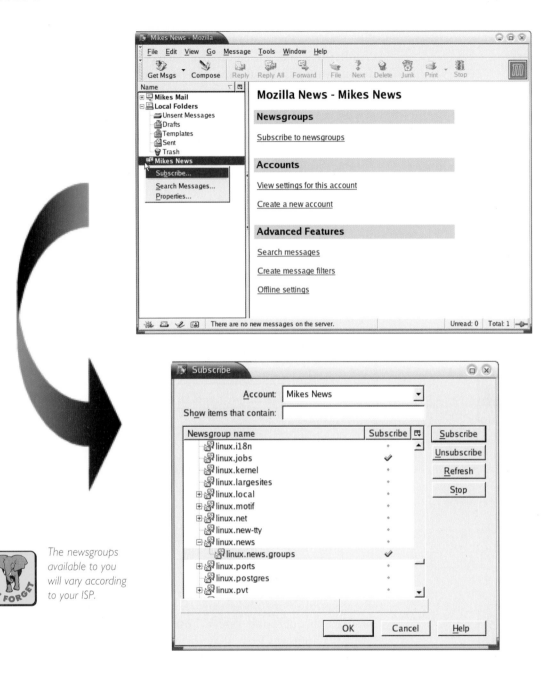

The newsgroups available to you will vary according to your ISP.

Click OK when you have made your selections and the chosen newsgroups appear under your news account menu in the left-hand pane – click any newsgroup to read the posted messages.

Transferring files

File Transfer Protocol (FTP) is a client-server protocol that enables files to be efficiently transferred around networks – such as the Internet and Local Area Network (LAN).

A public FTP site is hosted on a computer running FTP server software that is connected to the Internet. To access an FTP site you need to login using a password. Most public sites are accessible using a password of "anonymous" but private sites require a custom user name and password.

The pub directory is typically where files are stored which are intended for public access. A readme file or welcome file often provides information about the site.

The Mozilla web browser lets you browse public FTP sites graphically by automatically logging in as an anonymous user – just type `ftp://` followed by the site address into the URL field.

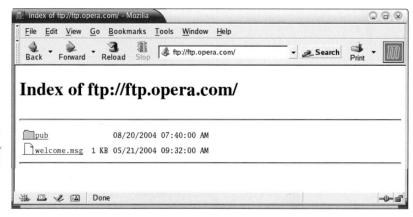

Where anonymous logins are not permitted Mozilla will simply state that it could not connect to the FTP site.

Double-click on the **pub** directory icon to open that directory and reveal the files and folders that it contains. Continue navigating through the FTP site until you reach the file/s you want to download.

See page 180 for details on installing downloaded packages.

For instance, the screenshot above illustrates the Opera FTP site where various versions of the Opera web browser are stored. Navigate through **pub**, **opera**, **linux** to reach the folders containing Linux versions of Opera that are available for download. Navigate further through the version and language sub-directories to reach the actual package file. Click on the preferred file to transfer it to your computer.

You may prefer not to use the command line, but it's sometimes very useful – in fact, its power can be addictive!

FTP file transfers can also be implemented from a command prompt in a console or shell window.

Type **ftp** at a prompt to launch the FTP program – the prompt changes to **ftp>**. Use the **open** command, followed by a space and the FTP address, to contact the FTP server there. When asked for a user name type **anonymous** for most public FTP sites. Typically, the server will then request you to enter your email address as a password.

There are many ftp commands – refer to the ftp manual page for a full list. See the Getting Help topic on page 64.

Once you are logged in, type the **ls** command to list the files and directories on the server. You can navigate through them using the **cd** command to change directory. When you locate a file that you wish to download use the **get** command, followed by a space and the file name, to copy the file to your computer.

The screenshot below illustrates how to login to the Opera web site from a command prompt. The welcome message is downloaded. Then the **more** command is used to read its contents. Finally, the **bye** command exits the FTP program.

The password has been entered but does not display on the screen for security reasons.

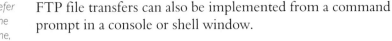

```
[mike]$ ftp
ftp> open ftp.opera.com
Connected to pub2.opera.com.
220 pub2.opera.com FTP server ready.
Name (ftp.opera.com:mike): anonymous
331 Anonymous login ok, send your complete email address as your password.
Password:
230-
230-Welcome to Opera Software's FTP service!
Using binary mode to transfer files.
ftp> ls
150 Opening ASCII mode data connection for file list
drwxr-xr-x    4 0        root           4096 Aug 20 07:40 pub
-rw-r--r--    1 0        root            273 May 21 09:32 welcome.msg
ftp> get welcome.msg
150 Opening BINARY mode data connection for welcome.msg (273 bytes).
226 Transfer complete.
ftp> bye
221 Goodbye.
[mike]$ more welcome.msg

Welcome to Opera Software's FTP service!

You are logged in as %U@%R

The time now is %T UTC

If you have any technical question about Opera, visit our support pages:

http://www.opera.com/support/

If you have problems with this FTP server, contact webmaster@opera.com.

[mike]$
```

Composing web pages

Mozilla includes a super free web page editor called Composer. This is a WYSIWYG (What You See Is What You Get) tool that lets you quickly create great-looking web pages.

Composer can be launched from Mozilla's Window menu, or from the component bar, or from the Start, Networking, WWW menu.

The Composer editor opens in "Normal" mode that allows you to create a page by adding content to its main window. Clicking tabs at the bottom of the window present different views of the page – "Preview" mode shows the page as it would look in a browser, "Source" mode reveals the actual HTML code and "Tags" mode adds HTML tag markers to the Normal mode view.

To control the flow of a page first create a table to hold the various contents – you can right-click on any cell and choose from the context menu to unite with other cells.

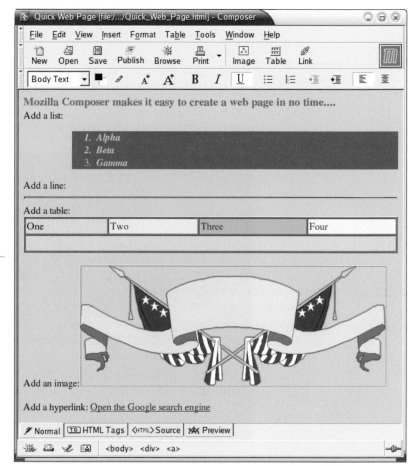

Text content can be added to the page by typing directly in or can be copy'n'pasted from another source. Drag the cursor over text to select it, then use the toolbar buttons to alter its size, color, font, highlight and position. Other toolbar buttons let you create bulleted or numbered lists with just one click.

Images, tables and hyperlinks can be added from the Insert menu or by clicking their toolbar equivalents. These each open a dialog to where you can specify explicit details – browse to the location of an image file, set the number of rows and columns for a table, enter the target URL for a hyperlink.

The properties of images, tables, lists and hyperlinks can be fine-tuned after they have been added to the page. Double-click on any one of these to open their Properties dialog box. Modify any of the basic properties in that dialog or click on the Advanced Edit button to edit more sophisticated properties of that item.

The screenshot below shows a simple JavaScript addition to an images onclick attribute – this will display an alert dialog if a user clicks that image when the page is displayed in a browser.

Composer will not run the JavaScript code – save the HTML file then open it in the Mozilla browser to try the script.

The string to be displayed in the alert dialog must be enclosed in single quotes to avoid conflict with the double quotes that surround the entire value – view this in Source mode to see how the code appears.

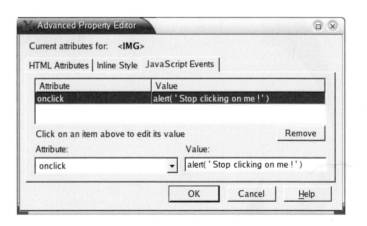

Messaging online

Linux includes several Instant Message clients. Typically, these can be found under the Start, Networking, Instant Messaging menu.

One of the most interesting IM tools is Gabber – the free open-source GNOME client for the Jabber instant messaging system. This does not rely on a single server and allows communication with other instant messaging systems, including ICQ and AIM.

Discover the latest news about Gabber, and find the online Gabber Manual at http://gabber.sourceforge.net.

The first time Gabber is launched a wizard asks you to create a new account. Enter the user name and password details then the wizard will login to Jabber. Click Add Contact on the Actions menu to add contacts to your roster, then click Send Message to open the message dialog where you can type and send your message.

Gabber also lets you chat online – click Join Group Chat, then select a chat room to enter.

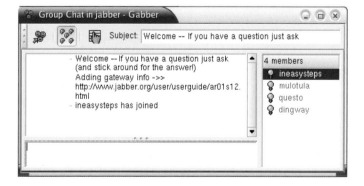

Touring the Linux file structure

The Linux directory structure is markedly different to that in Windows. This chapter begins by highlighting some of the fundamental differences between Linux and Windows then goes on to describe the hierarchical layout of Linux directories. The purpose of each standard Linux sub-directory is explained to illustrate how they are used. Demonstrations show how to navigate through the Linux directory structure – both in a graphical environment and from the command line.

Covers

The Linux directory tree | 82

Standard sub-directories | 84

Navigating with File Manager | 88

Navigating from the command line | 90

File system dos and don'ts | 92

Chapter Six

The Linux directory tree

When moving from Windows, the new Linux user needs to be aware of some fundamental differences between the two operating systems:

Discover more about access permissions in the next chapter.

- Linux is case-sensitive – Windows is not. For instance, a file named "readme.txt" and "README.txt" are seen as two distinctly different files in Linux, but there is no distinction in Windows

- Linux directories and files have ownership permissions that can restrict accessibility to the owner or group – Windows directories and files are generally universally accessible

- Linux was developed from the outset as a multi-user network operating system – Windows evolved from DOS as a single-user operating system intended for home use

- Linux users cannot change system settings, only the "root" super-user may do so – Windows desktop users have free reign

- Linux partitions are created using the Ext3 file system – Windows partitions use FAT, FAT32 or NTFS file systems

- Linux path names contain forward slash characters – Windows path names contain back slash characters. For instance, a Linux path **/usr/bin** and a Windows path **C:\mysql\bin**

- Linux does not have any drive letters – Windows typically uses A: for the floppy drive, C: for the hard disk drive, D: for the CD drive, and so on.

The lack of drive letters in Linux indicates what is, probably, the biggest difference between Linux and Windows – the way their directory structures are arranged. In Linux everything is contained within a single unified hierarchical system – beginning with the "root" directory, symbolized by a single forward slash "/".

Mandrake Linux automatically mounts the floppy and CD drives when it starts – other distros may not.

The Linux installation creates a number of standard sub-directories within the root directory. Each one of these, in turn, houses its own sub-directory structure, thereby creating a directory "tree" – the "root" directory is the root of the tree, as shown opposite.

Contents of peripheral drives appear in the tree in the directory at which they are "mounted" by Linux, creating a unified structure.

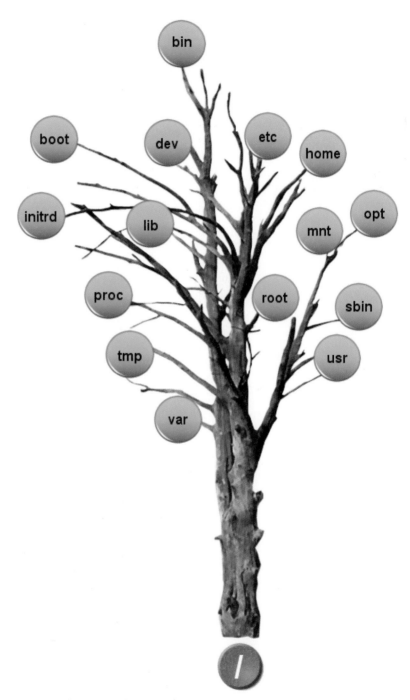

This illustration depicts typical standard sub-directories in Linux – the purpose of each directory is described on the following pages.

Do not confuse the "/" root directory with its "/root" sub-directory.

Standard sub-directories

/bin

Contains small executable programs (binaries) which are often considered to be part of the operating system itself – but they aren't really. For instance, when you type the **ls** command at a prompt, to list the contents of a directory, Linux executes the ls program that is located in the **/bin** directory. This directory is roughly equivalent to the **C:\Windows** directory in Windows.

/sbin

Contains executable system programs (binaries) that are only used by the root super-user and by Linux when the system is booting up or performing system recovery operations. For instance, the clock program that maintains the system time when Linux is running is located in the **/sbin** directory. This directory is roughly equivalent to the **C:\Windows\system** directory in Windows.

/lib

Contains binary library files which are used by the executable programs in the **/bin** and **/sbin** directories. These shared libraries are particularly important for booting the system and executing commands within the root file system. They are roughly equivalent to the DLL libraries in Windows but are not scattered around the system. Having a specific directory for support libraries avoids the common problem in Windows when multiple libraries have been installed and the system becomes confused about which one to use.

/dev

Contains special file system entries which represent devices that are attached to the system. These allow programs access to the device drivers which are essential for the system to function properly – although the actual driver files are located elsewhere. For instance, typically the entry **/dev/fd0** represents the floppy drive and the entry **/dev/cdrom0** represents the CD drive.

/boot

Contains the Linux kernel – the very heart of the operating system. Many people incorrectly use the term "operating system" to refer to the Linux environment but, strictly speaking, the kernel is the operating system. It is the program that controls access to all the hardware devices your computer supports and allows multiple programs to run concurrently and share that hardware. Typically the program is called "vmlinuz" – other programs that complement the kernel are located in the **/bin** and **/sbin** directories.

/etc

Contains system configuration files storing information about everything from user passwords and system initialization to screen resolution settings. All these are plain text files that can be viewed in any text editor, such as KEdit – there should never be any binary files in this directory. They control all configuration settings which are not user-specific. The files in this directory are roughly equivalent to the combination of **.ini** files and the Registry entries found in the Windows operating system.

/proc

Contains special files that relay information to and from the kernel. The hierarchy of "virtual" files within this directory represent the current state of the kernel – allowing applications and users to peer into the kernel's view of the system. For instance, at a command prompt type

```
more /proc/cpuinfo
```

to see information about your computer's processor/s. Similarly, typing the command

```
more /proc/meminfo
```

reveals information about your system's current memory usage. Unlike binary and text files, most virtual files are listed as zero bytes in size and are time stamped with the current date and time. This reflects the notion that they are constantly updating.

/mnt

Contains sub-directories that act as gateways to temporarily mounted file systems. This is the default location where most distros attach mounted file systems to the Linux directory tree. Typically, when peripheral drives have been mounted, the **/mnt/cdrom** directory lets you access files on a CD-ROM loaded in the CD drive and **/mnt/floppy** lets you access files on a floppy disk inserted in the floppy drive. On systems that dual-boot with Windows, **/mnt/windows** can reveal files on the Windows partition although accessibility can be restricted on NTFS file systems.

/usr

Contains sub-directories storing programs that can be run by any user of that system. For instance, games, word processors and media players. This directory is roughly equivalent to the **C:\Program Files** directory in Windows. The **/usr/local** sub-directory is intended for use by the system administrator, when installing software locally, to prevent it being overwritten when the system software is updated.

/var

Contains variable data files that store information about ongoing system status, particularly logs of system activity. The system administrator (superuser) can type the following command at a root prompt to see the record of system activity messages:

```
more /var/log/messages
```

/home

Contains a sub-directory for each user account to store personal data files. If there is a user account named "fred" there will be a **/home/fred** directory where that user can store personal files – other users cannot save files there. This directory is where you store all your working documents, images and media files and is the rough equivalent of the **My Documents** directory in the Windows operating system.

/tmp

Contains, as you might expect, temporary files that have been created by running programs. Mostly these are deleted when the program gets closed but some do get left behind – periodically these should be deleted. This directory is roughly equivalent to the **C:\Windows\Temp** directory in Windows.

/root

This is the home directory for the root account superuser – for security reasons regular users cannot access this directory. If you login to Linux as root and open that account's home directory it's at **/root**, rather than a sub-directory of **/home** like regular users.

/initrd

Contains only a text file warning that this directory should not be deleted. It is used during the boot process to mount the Linux file system itself. Removing this directory will leave the computer unable to boot Linux – instead it will generate a "kernel panic" error message.

/opt

Contains nothing initially, but this directory provides a special area where large static application software packages can be installed. A package placing files in **/opt** creates a sub-directory bearing the same name as the package. This sub-directory contains files that would otherwise be scattered around the file system, giving the system administrator an easy way to determine the role of each file. For instance, if "example" is the name of a particular software package in the **/opt** directory, then all its files could be placed within sub-directories of the **/opt/example** directory – binaries in **/opt/example/bin**, manual pages in **/opt/example/man**, and so on. The entire application can be easily removed by deleting the **/opt/example** directory – along with all its sub-directories and files.

Navigating with File Manager

To graphically view the standard sub-directories within the root directory launch the Konqueror browser, then type a forward slash in the location field and hit Return.

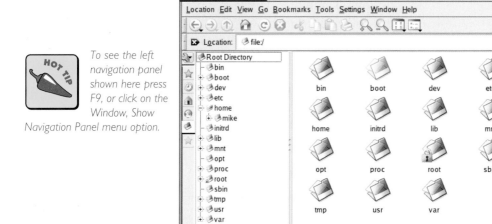

To see the left navigation panel shown here press F9, or click on the Window, Show Navigation Panel menu option.

Notice in the screenshot above that the icon of the sub-directory called **/root** includes a lock graphic – indicating that it is not accessible to regular users. To have full accessibility launch the File Manager application from Start, Applications, File Tools, File Manager – Super User Mode. This emulates the root super-user and allows greater control of the file system.

You can drag'n'drop files from the desktop into directories shown in the File Manager window.

Go to the **/** location and notice that the **/root** directory is no longer locked. Click the View menu, then select the Folder Icons Reflect Contents option to usefully mark the folder icons with graphics that indicate their contents.

The icon size in the right-hand pane can be adjusted by clicking the "zoom" buttons on the toolbar. Alternatively click the View menu, then select the Icon Size option and choose one of the pre-determined icon sizes.

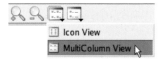

The contents of the right-hand pane can be presented in a variety of ways by holding down the mouse on either of the "view" buttons and selecting one of the menu options.

You can navigate through the file system in File Manager by clicking on a folder in the right-hand pane, or by clicking on a directory in the navigation panel, or by typing its name in the location field and pressing the Return key. For instance, navigate to the **/bin** directory where many of the Linux executables are stored.

Shortcuts are marked with an arrow – as they are in Windows.

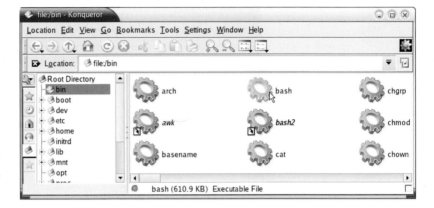

Position the pointer over a file graphic and information describing that file is displayed on the window's status bar – the screenshot above shows the bash program, used frequently as the Linux shell.

 Navigation buttons on the toolbar allow you to easily move forward, backward and up to a higher directory level.

Most often you will want to work in the **/home** directory, which can be reached by any of the usual methods, or by simply clicking the "home" button on the toolbar when not in Super User Mode.

The home button in Super User Mode takes you to /root, not to /home – /root is the root user's home directory.

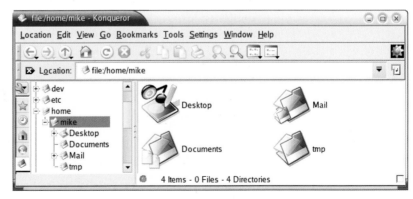

Navigating from the command line

To view the standard sub-directories within the root directory from the command line first type **cd /** to change into the root directory. Then type **ls** and hit Return to list the contents.

 The prompt illustrated here includes the user's name but other prompts may not – type **whoami** *at a prompt to reveal your user name.*

As in Windows, directories can contain "hidden" files that usually store configuration information – in Linux hidden file names begin with a dot. To include hidden files in the listing of directory content add the **-a** argument after the **ls** command.

 Type **date** *at a prompt to see the current system date and time information.*

Navigate to any immediate sub-directory by typing **cd** followed by a space and the directory name. In the screenshot below the user first opens the **/home** standard sub-directory and lists the contents, then opens the next-level sub-directory named **mike** and lists its contents – in this case four sub-directories.

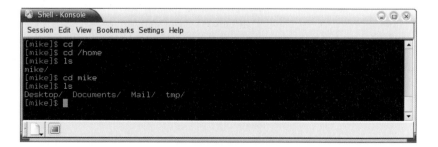

...cont'd

As an alternative to drilling down through each sub-directory in turn you can navigate to any location in the file system by stating its full path from root. For instance, in the screenshot below the user navigates directly from **/** to the **/Documents** directory of the **/mike** user directory, located in the **/home** standard sub-directory.

Remember that Linux is case-sensitive when typing the Documents path.

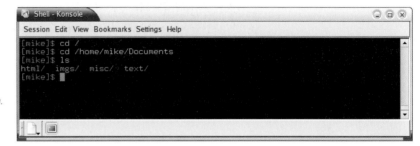

It is sometimes easy to forget at what location in the file system you are working. Type the command **pwd** to print the working directory – this gives the full path of your current location.

You can navigate to the next higher level directory using **cd ..** and, usefully, the **/home** directory in Linux can also be referred to by its short name of **~** , using just the tilde character.

*Notice how the user navigates two levels down from the **mike** directory using a relative path – the alternative using an absolute path is **cd /home/mike/Documents/text**.*

File system dos and don'ts

When organizing your files and directories in Linux it is advisable to adopt the recommendations listed below. These conform to accepted standards of practice and make working in Linux easier:

1   Never place files directly in the root directory ("/") and never create directories there – the top-level root directory should only ever contain the standard Linux sub-directories.

File extensions are unimportant in Linux – but if you're coming from a Windows background, use them to help readily identify the file types.

2   Always use your personal home directory to store all your personal data files – for instance, the **/home/mike** directory. Create as many sub-directories as you like in your home directory, but do not store data files elsewhere.

3   Use only lowercase when naming any data files you create as this prevents any possible future hassle with capitalization errors. For instance, you won't have to remember if you named a file **Mydata**, **MYDATA** or **MyData** – it will always simply be **mydata**.

Recommendations on this page are not mandatory – but experienced Linux users may expect you to adhere to them.

4   When naming files avoid using any spaces in the name. Linux can easily cope with these in graphical mode but it can create a problem in text mode – you will have to remember to prefix each space in the name with a "\" backslash character when referencing that file from the command line. It is much simpler to simply avoid spaces.

5   Only use the root superuser account whenever it is absolutely necessary. If you are logged in as root remember that you have absolute power – and, therefore, the ability to wreak havoc. Get into the habit of working from a regular user account.

Handling files

This chapter illustrates how to create and manipulate files in Linux. The concept of file ownership is explained and examples demonstrate how to change file permissions. It also shows how to access files on Windows from within Mandrake Linux.

Covers

Creating a new text file | 94

Moving files around | 96

Deleting files | 98

Making shortcuts | 100

Changing access permissions | 102

Accessing files in Windows | 104

Compressing and extracting files | 106

Getting better compression | 108

Chapter Seven

Creating a new text file

To create a text file in KDE first open one of the editor applications. For instance, click on Start, Applications, Editors then choose the KEdit (Text Editor) option to launch the KEdit editor.

To change the appearance of KEdit click on the Settings menu and select the Configure KEdit option – choose your font, colors, spellchecker and word wrap preferences.

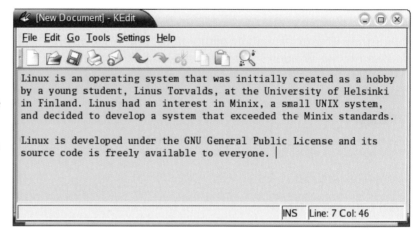

Type text content directly into the KEdit window then click on File, Save to open the Save File As dialog box. Enter a directory in the topmost field to determine where the file should be saved – you can click on the arrowed button then select a directory from the drop-down list that appears. Enter a name for the file in the "Location:" field, then click the OK button to save the file.

The left-hand pane provides location options that you can click to quickly select where to save the new text file.

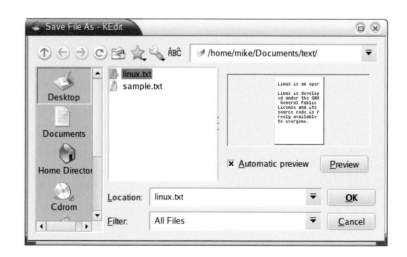

The Edit menu has all the usual options to cut, copy, paste, find and replace text and the Go menu lets you move to a specified line number. To check for spelling errors in the text click the Tools menu and select the Spelling option to run the Spellcheck.

You can choose which locale dictionary the Spellcheck should use – click Settings, Configure KEdit to launch the Configure dialog box, then click the Spelling option.

The Portable Document Format (PDF) was developed by Adobe Systems. They are compact files that maintain the original document format for viewing and printing.

Click on File, Print to open the Print dialog – the arrowed button in the "Name:" field reveals a drop-down list of great options. Besides allowing a printer to produce a hard copy you can create a PDF or PostScript version of your text document. Additionally, the Mail PDF File option opens the default email application with a PDF version of the text document already attached and ready to go.

Discover how to create and edit text files from the command prompt with the vi editor examples on page 152.

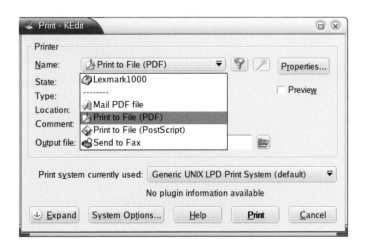

Moving files around

Use Konqueror to graphically cut, or copy, files to the Linux clipboard then paste them into another directory. Right-click on the file to move, then choose the Cut or Copy option from the context menu that appears.

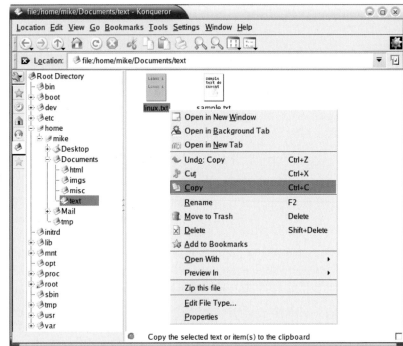

Notice that the context menu has options to open the document in a tabbed window – KEdit can simultaneously work with several text documents, each in its own tabbed window.

In the navigation panel, right-click on the target directory then choose Paste from the context menu to move the file, or to create a duplicate when copying.

Konqueror also lets you drag'n'drop files from one directory to another. Open the source directory so its files appear in the right-hand pane. Left-click on the file you want to move and hold down the left mouse button. Drag the pointer across to the target directory in the left-hand navigation panel then release the mouse button. A context menu will appear – choose the Move Here option to cut'n'paste the file, or choose the Copy Here option to copy'n'paste the file.

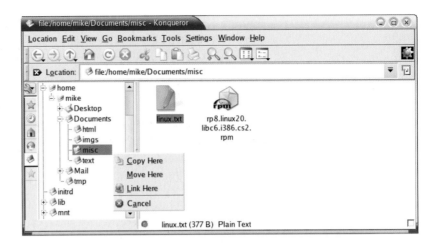

*To rename a file select the Rename option on the context menu then type its new name in the dialog that appears. Or use the **mv** command to rename a file at a prompt with the syntax* **mv** *oldname newname.*

Moving files to another location from the command line is achieved using the **mv** command. This must be followed by a space and the file name, then the target directory path.

Similarly, files can be copied to another directory using the **cp** command with the same syntax. For instance, the user in the screenshot below copies the text file named **linux.txt** from the **/text** directory to the adjacent **/misc** directory.

```
[mike]$ cd /home/mike/Documents/text
[mike]$ pwd
/home/mike/Documents/text
[mike]$ ls
linux.txt   sample.txt
[mike]$ cp linux.txt ../misc
[mike]$ cd ../misc
[mike]$ pwd
/home/mike/Documents/misc
[mike]$ ls
linux.txt
[mike]$ ▪
```

Deleting files

Launch Konqueror and navigate to a location in your home directory. Right-click in the window to open the context menu and select the Create New Directory option. Enter a name, such as "temp", then click the OK button to create the directory.

Place a text file in the new directory – write a new file or copy'n'paste an existing one. Now right-click on the new directory to open a context menu that provides two options to remove it.

The first option, to Move To Trash, will move the directory, and any folders it contains, to the Trash Bin. This is a holding area from which directories and files can be recovered if desired. The second option, to Delete, will remove the directory and its files permanently – they cannot be recovered.

The context menu lets you remove directories that are not empty without question – always use the Move To Trash option unless you are absolutely certain you will never want to recover any of its contents.

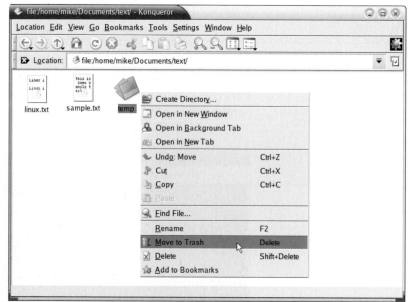

To recover items from Trash open Konqueror at the location to which you want them to be restored then click on the Trash Bin icon on the desktop. Cut'n'paste, or drag'n'drop, the directory or file/s from the Trash into the required location.

To permanently delete files and directories from Trash right-click on the Trash icon and select the Empty Trash Bin option.

Deleting files and directories from the command line provides more safeguards against accidental deletion by requiring confirmation of those actions before they are implemented.

To reproduce the example on the opposite page at the command line navigate to a location in your home directory then type **mkdir**, followed by a space and a name, to create a new directory. Copy a file into the new directory then type **rmdir** and the directory name to attempt to delete the directory and its contents.

Use the wildcard * *to delete all files with the command* **rm** *.*

Linux will not allow non-empty directories to be deleted – you must first open the directory and delete its contents using the **rm** command. Linux will request you type **y** (yes) to confirm this action then it will permanently delete the file/s. Now move up to the higher level directory using **cd ..** and issue the **rmdir** command once more to delete the empty directory.

```
[mike]$ cd /home/mike/Documents/text
[mike]$ pwd
/home/mike/Documents/text
[mike]$ ls
linux.txt   sample.txt
[mike]$ mkdir temp
[mike]$ ls
linux.txt   sample.txt   temp/
[mike]$ cp sample.txt temp
[mike]$ cd temp
[mike]$ ls
sample.txt
[mike]$ cd..
[mike]$ rmdir temp
rmdir: `temp': Directory not empty
[mike]$ cd temp
[mike]$ rm sample.txt
rm: remove regular file `sample.txt'? y
[mike]$ cd..
[mike]$ rmdir temp
[mike]$ ls
linux.txt   sample.txt
[mike]$
```

The command **rmdir -rf** *is highly dangerous – vast areas of your file system can be permanently deleted at a stroke. It is best avoided.*

Some Linux distributions allow non-empty directories to be deleted, along with their entire contents, by including a **-rf** argument (recursive, force) in the **rmdir** command. For instance, the command **rmdir -rf temp** could instantly and permanently delete the directory named **temp** and all sub-directories and files within it.

Making shortcuts

It is often convenient to create desktop shortcuts to the applications and files that you access most frequently. To create a new desktop shortcut to an application first find it on the Start menu, then drag'n'drop it onto the desktop.

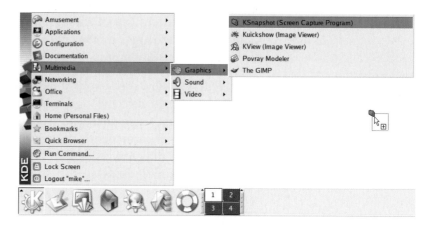

Release the mouse button then select the Link Here option from the context menu that appears – an icon gets added to the desktop which you can click to launch that application.

The KSnapshot application, to which this shortcut links, was used to grab the screenshots that appear throughout this book.

KSnapshot

To create a desktop shortcut to a file drag'n'drop it onto the desktop from Konqueror then choose Link Here – an icon gets added to the desktop which you can click to open that file.

sample.txt

Notice that the file name is italicized under both shortcuts to denote that these are merely pointers – not actual locations.

In Linux these type of shortcuts are known as "symbolic links" or "symlinks", and sometimes as "soft links". When you click on this type of link it operates on the original file to which it points. There can be multiple symbolic links, all pointing to the same original file. If the original file gets deleted the links point to an empty location so the shortcuts no longer work.

Hard links can only be made to files on the same file system – soft links can be made to files on remote systems, such as the URL of a web page on the Internet.

Linux also allows the creation of "hard links". This type of link creates a copy of the original file, but in another location. When you click on this type of link it operates on the copy file and also updates the original file to be identical. There can be multiple hard links, all getting updated whenever changes are made to any one of them. If the original file gets deleted the hard links continue to work until the final one is deleted from the system.

To make a hard link to a file right-click on the desktop then click on the Create New menu and select the Link To Location option.

sample.txt

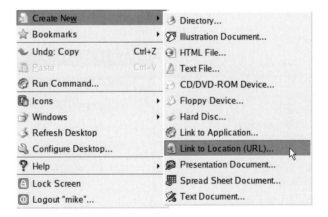

A symbolic link is just a pointer, whereas a hard link is an actual file – normally use symbolic links to create desktop shortcuts to your files and apps.

In the dialog that appears browse to the file to which you want to hard link then click the OK button – an icon gets added to the desktop displaying the same file name as that to which it is linked.

Click on the desktop hard link file and it will open to reveal identical contents to the original file. Add some content then save the hard link file. Now open the original file and notice that it too contains the added content. Delete the original file and see that you can still open the intact hard link file on the desktop.

Changing access permissions

In Linux each file and directory has an "owner" – typically this is the user who created it. The owner has full permission to read the file, write to the file and to execute the file (if it's executable).

An executable file is a binary program file that can be "run" – a text file is not an executable file.

The owner may also set permissions to specify if other users can read, write and execute the file. The file's accessibility can be restricted to the owner, or to a "group" of which the owner is a member, or to any user of the system.

To view the permission settings of a file in KDE right-click on it, select Properties from the context menu, then click the Permissions tab in the Properties dialog that appears.

Usually the User, Group and Others will have permission to at least Read the file. If you are the owner of the file the User will have permission to Write and Execute the file (if it's executable).

As the owner of the file you can check any unchecked boxes to extend the permissions of this file – click the OK button to apply the new permission settings.

Ignore the checkboxes under the Special heading – these are used to set unique numerical identification numbers to avoid file conflicts across multiple file systems.

To view the permission settings of a file at the command line use the **ls** command with its **-l** option to get a long listing – type **ls -l** then hit Return.

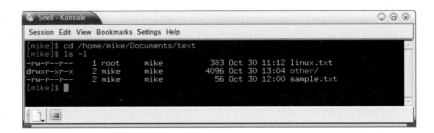

The long listing line also shows the number of hard links, the owner, group, file size and date/time of creation.

The long listing of each line begins with a string of 10 characters – the first is a "d" for a directory, or a dash for a file. This is followed by sequential Read, Write and Execute permissions for the owning User, Group and Others. Characters "r", "w" and "x" appear for those permissions that are set – otherwise a dash is shown.

Each set of permissions can also be described numerically where Read = 4, Write = 2 and Execute = 1. For instance, a value of 7 describes full permissions to Read, Write and Execute (4 + 2 + 1), a value of 6 describes permissions to Read, Write (4 + 2), a value of 5 describes Write, Execute permissions (4 + 1), and so on.

Permissions can be changed from the command line using the **chmod** command. This needs two further arguments stating the permission values and the file name. The owner could, for example, type the command **chmod 777 myfile** to set full permissions for a file named **myfile** in the current directory.

*Type **exit** to logout of root and return to a regular user prompt.*

If you need to change permissions where you are not the owner you need Super-user power – in KDE you can use Applications, File Tools, File Manager - Super User Mode and just make changes in the Permissions dialog as shown opposite. Alternatively, at a command prompt type **su** then enter the root password if asked – the style of the prompt will change to the root prompt.

*Read the man pages for more on the **chmod** command. Also check out the **chown** command that lets root change ownership of a file.*

Accessing files in Windows

On dual-boot systems the Windows partition may be mounted in Linux to allow a degree of access to the files stored there. This process is similar to the way that peripheral drives are mounted – allowing access to files on portable media, such as CD-ROMs.

User-friendly Linux distros, such as Mandrake Linux, automatically mount the Windows partition for you. This means you can easily access the files in Windows from the **/mnt/windows** directory in Linux.

This example shows one of the sample images supplied with Photoshop (on the Windows partition) being readily accessed from Linux.

Older Windows 9.x operating systems use the FAT or FAT32 file system which Linux can both read from, and write to. Modern Windows platforms, such as XP, use the NTFS file system which can be less simple – some Linux distros do not support NTFS so cannot access the Windows partition at all. Other distros, such as Mandrake Linux, may be able to read from NTFS but not write to it – check your distro's documentation to see if it supports NTFS.

Where Linux cannot directly write to the Windows partition you can copy files into Linux for modification then save them on portable media, such as a CD-ROM or floppy disk – now boot Windows and copy the modified files back in.

If your Linux distro does not automatically mount the Windows partition you may need to do so manually. First determine the physical location of the Windows partition – if it's at the start of the first HD drive it will probably be **/dev/hda1**. Use the Control Center to confirm the location – for instance, in RedHat Linux open the Hardware Browser and select Hard Drives.

At a command prompt type **su**, then enter the root password to login to the root account. Now create a directory in which the Windows partition can be mounted using this command

```
mkdir /mnt/windows
```

To mount the Windows partition in this new directory, type the following command (where **/dev/hda1** is the Windows partition):

```
mount -t vfat /dev/hda1 /mnt/windows
```

Type **exit** to logout of the root account and access your Windows data by changing into the mounted Windows partition:

```
cd /mnt/windows
```

You will need to modify the line to reflect the location of the Windows partition if not /dev/hda1 – and the file system if not vfat.

To automatically mount a Windows partition every time Linux boots you can modify the **/etc/fstab** file, which configures all file systems and disk device mounting options. Open this file in a text editor, such as KEdit, and add the following line then save the file.

```
/dev/hda1 /mnt/windows vfat auto,umask=0 0 0
```

Now whenever Linux is booted, the **/etc/fstab** file is read, and the Windows partition gets automatically mounted in **/mnt/windows**.

Compressing and extracting files

Files in Linux, and other Unix-based operating systems, are typically archived into a "tarball" for compact transfer. This first creates a Tape ARchive (TAR) copy of the files then compresses that copy using the familiar ZIP compression format.

TAR was originally used for backing up files on tape in a manner that preserves the file permissions and hierarchy.

In KDE right-click on a directory folder to be archived then select the "Tar this directory" option on the context menu. A tarball version of the directory and its contents are created in the current location – this has the same name, but adds a **.tar.gz** extension.

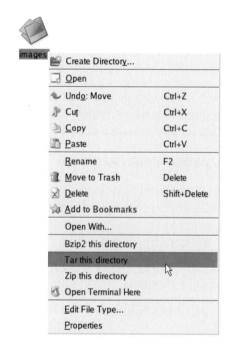

images.tar.gz

*The ZIP tool in Linux is called GZip – hence the **.gz** part of the file extension of the tarball archive.*

To extract the contents of a tarball in KDE right-click on the file then select the "Extract here" option from the context menu. The application associated with archives will then deposit all the expanded file contents in the current directory location.

Alternatively, choose the Open With context menu option and select the archive tool you would prefer to extract the contents. This allows specific files to be selected for extraction from within the tarball and lets you choose a destination other than the current location.

The tar program has many options – it's common to add the **v** option for verbose output. Read the tar manual pages for the full list of options.

The tar program can be used at the command line with its **cf** (create file) option to archive a directory or file/s. For instance, the following command creates an archive called **images.tar** from a directory **/imgs** that contains some image files.

```
tar cf images.tar imgs
```

You can list the contents of an existing archive with the **tf** option, such as **tar tf images.tar**. And the contents of an archive can be extracted into the current directory with the **xf** option, such as **tar xf images.tar**.

The GZip program can be used at the command line to compress an individual file or tar archive. For example, the command

```
gzip images.tar
```

compresses a tar archive to produce a tarball named **images.tar.gz**. Similarly, a compressed file can be uncompressed with the gunzip command – **gunzip images.tar.gz** reduces the tarball to a tar archive once more.

The archiving and compression operations can be combined by adding the **z** option to the other tar options – so, for instance

```
tar cfz images.tar.gz imgs
```

creates a tar archive then compresses it to produce the tarball named **images.tar.gz** of the **/imgs** directory and all its contents. The **tfz** options list the tarball's contents and the **xfz** options will extract all the contents into the current directory.

Extract a specific file from a tarball by adding its file name to the end of the extraction command – or specify multiple files as a space-separated list.

```
[mike]$ pwd
/home/mike/Documents
[mike]$ ls
html/   imgs/   misc/   text/
[mike]$ tar cfz images.tar.gz imgs
[mike]$ ls
html/   images.tar.gz   imgs/   misc/   text/
[mike]$ tar tfz images.tar.gz
imgs/
imgs/jester.gif
imgs/banner.gif
imgs/linux.jpg
[mike]$
```

Getting better compression

Many Linux distros include an alternative to the GZip compression tool called Bzip2. This can often produce smaller tarball files because it uses better compression techniques.

Right-click on a directory to archive and compress, then select the Bzip2 option from the context menu – shown on page 106. The tarball is created in the current directory with the directory name and an added file extension of **tar.bz2**.

In the screenshot below tarballs have been created of the **/imgs** directory using both GZip and Bzip2. The original directory size of 4.6Mb is compressed to 3.6Mb by GZip but to 3.2Mb by Bzip2.

Although Bzip2 enjoys widespread support it is not as ubiquitous as the regular ZIP compression format – most tarballs for download are still GZipped archives.

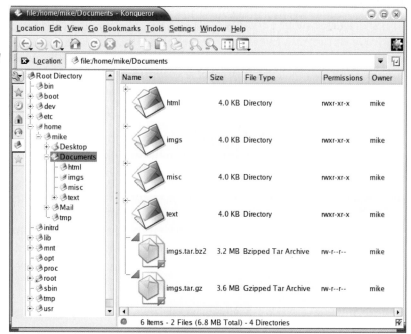

The Bzip2 program can also be used at the command line to compress an individual file or tar archive. For example, the command `bzip2 images.tar` compresses a tar archive to produce a tarball named **images.tar.bz2**. Similarly, a compressed file can be uncompressed with the `bunzip2` command – `bunzip2 images.tar.gz` reduces the tarball to a tar archive.

Working in a Linux office suite

This chapter describes the features of the free OpenOffice suite that is widely used in Linux. It examines how this open-source application fares against the market-leading Microsoft Office product and illustrates some additional benefits of OpenOffice.

Covers

Introducing the OpenOffice suite | 110

Documents in OpenOffice Writer | 111

Exporting documents from OpenOffice | 112

Spreadsheets in OpenOffice Calc | 114

Presentations in OpenOffice Impress | 116

Charts and graphs in OpenOffice Draw | 118

Formulas in OpenOffice Math | 120

Chapter Eight

Introducing the OpenOffice suite

The OpenOffice suite is an application containing a set of office tools similar to those in Microsoft Office. It is based on original code from the StarOffice application by Sun MicroSystems. Sun made the code freely available for development by the open-source community so OpenOffice has no proprietary ties. The splash screen that displays when OpenOffice is launched does, however, acknowledge this heritage.

OpenOffice is included with most Linux distros. It can also be freely downloaded from www.openoffice.org – clear installation instructions are provided on the website too.

There are versions of OpenOffice available for many platforms, including Linux, Mac OS X and Windows.

OpenOffice comprises word processor ("Writer"), spreadsheet ("Calc"), and presentation ("Impress") programs that are similar to the Word, Excel and PowerPoint programs in MS Office. It also has a program, to create charts, graphs and diagrams ("Draw"), and a specialized tool for formatting mathematical formulas ("Math"). If you are familiar with MS Office you will feel instantly at home with the OpenOffice equivalents.

Most importantly, OpenOffice contains file filters that allow it to work with standard MS Office documents from Word, Excel and PowerPoint. Files can be saved in MS Office file formats, as well as formats native to OpenOffice.

It can embed objects (OLE objects, plugins, video, applets, charts) within a document – but using these advanced features may create issues when trying to share the document with another office suite. For instance, an OpenOffice document containing an embedded spreadsheet works fine in OpenOffice, but the spreadsheet may not be displayed when that document is viewed in MS Word.

Documents in OpenOffice Writer

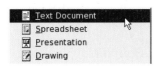

Launch OpenOffice then click the File, New menu to be presented with a sub-menu of possible document types – for regular word processing choose the Text Document option. A new blank document then appears where you can position the cursor and begin typing text content.

You can modify the appearance of selected text using the options on the Object Bar to change the font, size, style, decoration, weight, alignment, color and background color. Automatic numbering or bullets may also be added to list items.

The Insert menu has options to add graphics, hyperlinks, tables and OLE objects into the document.

Function Bar ——

Object Bar ——

Main Toolbar ——

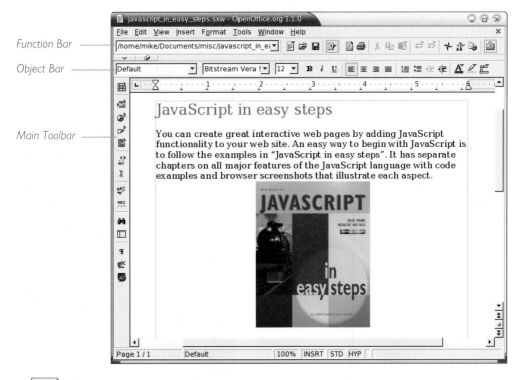

javascript_in_
easy_steps.sxw

Click on the File, Save menu to save the document at a suitable location in your home directory. This will open the Save As dialog where you can enter a file name – by default the document will be saved in the OpenOffice native format with a **.sxw** extension.

Exporting documents from OpenOffice

In order to save a document for use in MS Office choose the File, Save As menu in OpenOffice, then select the **.doc** file format in the Save As dialog.

The screenshots below show the document from the previous page being saved to a floppy disk for use in MS Office. When this gets opened in MS Word the text content and graphic are preserved but the text appears in Word's default "Times New Roman" font.

javascript_in_
easy_steps.doc

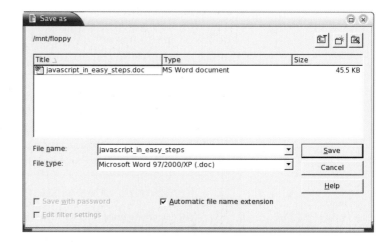

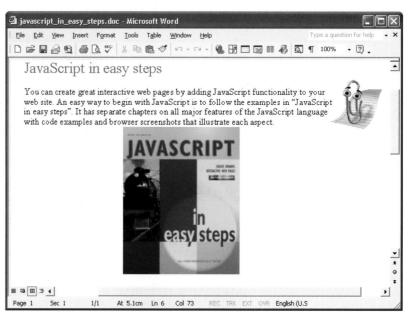

One real bonus in OpenOffice is the built-in support for the Portable Document Format. This allows you to create read-only versions of your documents in the popular PDF format without any additional costly software. The PDF format maintains the style and content of the original document in a very compact file that can be easily transferred around networks and the Internet.

To export a PDF version of your document from OpenOffice click the File, Export As PDF menu – or click the "Export Directly As PDF" button on the Function Bar. Either will open the Export dialog (similar to the Save As dialog shown opposite) where you can choose a file name and location for the PDF file.

javascript_in_
easy_steps.pdf

For instance, exporting a PDF version of the original document shown on page 111 to a floppy disk creates a file there with the **.pdf** extension. The screenshot below illustrates that file opened on a Windows platform in the Internet Explorer browser – using the Adobe Reader plugin. Notice that the text closely maintains the font appearance of that in the original document.

The OpenOffice file filters allow documents to be saved in many other formats including HTML (.html) and plain text (.txt) – the HTML file format creates copies of embedded images for display in that HTML document, whereas the plain text file format loses all images and style formatting.

Spreadsheets in OpenOffice Calc

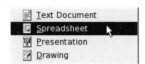

Launch OpenOffice then click the File, New menu to be presented with a sub-menu of possible document types – for spreadsheets choose the Spreadsheet option. A new blank spreadsheet comprising cells, arranged in rows and columns, then appears where you can position the cursor and enter content.

Click on a cell and enter text that can be a heading or descriptive label for the spreadsheet's content. Enter numeric data in cells that you wish to contain the actual content and include a currency symbol if the data is of monetary value – this ensures that the value is shown with two decimal places. For instance, type **$5** then select another cell to apply the entry – the value appears as $5.00.

The data in the spreadsheet below describes a table of expenditure over a 4-week period.

Formula Bar

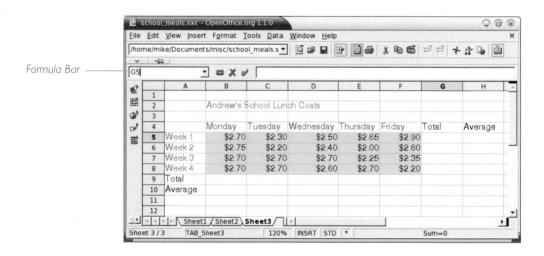

To quickly see the total of all values in a column or row click on the gray column heading letter button, or gray row number button, and its sum total instantly appears in the status bar as "Sum = " result.

The power of spreadsheets lies in their ability to perform calculations on their data entries using given formulas. For instance, to total the expenditure for Week 1 in the above example click in the Total cell on that row, then type **=** – the symbol appears in that cell and also in the input field on the Formula Bar. Now add the formula, in either that cell or the input field. In this case it is the sum of the cells of each day on the Week 1 row – so you would type **B5+C5+D5+E5+F5**. Hit the Return key to apply the formula and the sum total value appears in the Total cell.

Alternatively a total value can be ascertained using the SUM() function. Type **=S** in the Total cell and a tooltip appears prompting you to use the SUM() function. Hit the Return key, to confirm you want to use this function, then select the cells whose values you wish to total – in the example above these are cells B5,C5,D5,E5 and F5. The formula appears in the cell, and the Formula Bar input field, as **=SUM(B5:F5)**. Hit the Return key to apply the formula and the total value appears in the Total cell.

Similarly, the AVERAGE() function can be used in exactly the same way to calculate the average of a range of values. Type **=A** in the Average cell and a tooltip appears prompting you to use the AVERAGE() function. Hit the Return key, then highlight the cells whose values you wish to average. Hit the Return key again to apply the formula and the average value appears in the Average cell.

Applying formulas across the example quickly creates totals and averages for each week and each day. Right-click on a range of cells and choose the Format Cells option on the context menu and choose a background color to highlight the data in those cells.

Formula Bar buttons can apply formulas to rows. Select an empty cell at the end of a row then click the **∑** *Formula button – a suggested formula appears in the input field and the button is replaced by "Accept" and "Cancel" buttons. Click the* ✔ *"Accept" button to apply the formula.*

The "light bulb" in bottom right corner of this illustration is the Open Office Help Agent – check the Help file for the full range of spreadsheet functions for OpenOffice Calc.

	school_meals.sxc - OpenOffice.org 1.1.0							
File Edit View Insert Format Tools Data Window Help								
/home/mike/Documents/misc/school_meals.s ▼								
H10		▼	∑ =	=AVERAGE(H5:H8)				
	A	B	C	D	E	F	G	H
1								
2		Andrew's School Lunch Costs						
3								
4		Monday	Tuesday	Wednesday	Thursday	Friday	Total	Average
5	Week 1	$2.70	$2.30	$2.50	$2.65	$2.90	$13.05	$2.61
6	Week 2	$2.75	$2.20	$2.40	$2.00	$2.60	$11.95	$2.39
7	Week 3	$2.70	$2.70	$2.70	$2.25	$2.35	$12.70	$2.54
8	Week 4	$2.70	$2.70	$2.60	$2.70	$2.20	$12.90	$2.58
9	Total	$10.85	$9.90	$10.20	$9.60	$10.05	$50.60	
10	Average	$2.71	$2.48	$2.55	$2.40	$2.51		$2.53
11								
12								
Sheet1 \ **Sheet2** / Sheet3								
Sheet 2 / 3	TAB_Sheet2		120%		STD		Sum=$2.53	

school_meals.
SXC

To save the spreadsheet click on the File, Save As menu and type a name for the file in the Save As dialog – the native file format for OpenOffice Calc adds the file extension **.sxc**. Choose the file format **.xls** if you want the spreadsheet to work with Excel in the MS Office suite.

Presentations in OpenOffice Impress

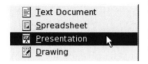

Launch OpenOffice then click the File, New menu to be presented with a sub-menu of possible document types – for slide show presentations choose the Presentation option. An "AutoPilot" wizard dialog appears where you can choose to create a presentation from scratch, use a supplied template, or open an existing presentation for editing.

To start a new presentation check "Empty Presentation", then click the Next button to see a choice of backgrounds – a preview is shown of each option when it is selected. Choose a preference, then click the Next button to proceed. A number of transitional effects are available in a drop-down list – choose your preference if you want your slide to fade in, then click the Create button to open the Modify Slide dialog.

Click the layout option most suitable for the content you wish to display on the slide, then click the OK button to close the dialog. The chosen layout is applied to the slide, and you can now click each part to add the actual content.

To run a spelling check on text in any OpenOffice window click the Check option on the Spellcheck sub-menu (under the Tools menu) – or just hit the F7 key on your keyboard.

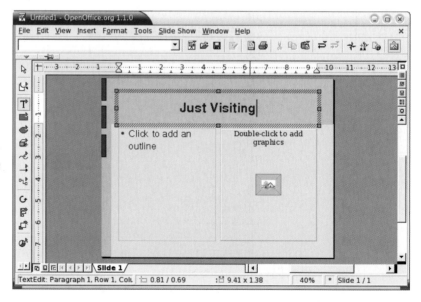

The appearance of selected text can be modified using options on the right-click context menu, or from the Format menu. For instance, select some text to modify then click the Character sub-menu. Now you can adjust the Font, Font Effects and Position of the selected text in the Character dialog.

Animated effects can be applied to blocks of text in the Text dialog found on the context menu – but these should be used sparingly.

When you're happy with the way the slide looks choose the Slide, Insert Slide option from the context menu to add another slide to the presentation. Repeat the process of layout selection, adding content and formatting to the new slide.

To run the slide show select the bottom tab of the first slide, then right-click and select the Slide Show option on the context menu – click on each slide, or use the Return key, to advance.

The slide show can also be started with the F9 key, or with the Slide Show option on the Slide Show menu.

The slides can be made to advance automatically by specifying timer options in the Slide Show Settings dialog – found on the Slide Show menu.

comedy_
movies.sxi

To save the presentation click on the File, Save As menu and type a name for the file in the Save As dialog – the native file format for OpenOffice Impress adds the file extension **.sxi**. Choose the file format **.ppt** if you want the presentation to work with PowerPoint in the MS Office suite.

Charts and graphs in OpenOffice Draw

Launch OpenOffice then click the File, New menu to be presented with a sub-menu of possible document types – for charts, graphs and other graphics choose the Drawing option. A blank drawing area appears where a range of vector graphics can be created.

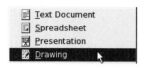

The main toolbar down the left side of the window contains a series of buttons depicting predefined vector objects. Click and hold down the mouse button on any one of these to open a small window showing a number of associated options. For instance, the 3D object button offers a cube, cone, sphere, cylinder, and so on.

Click on any shape to select it then drag the cursor in the drawing area to create that object. As with other vector graphic programs selected objects have handles that allow you to adjust their size. Click an existing object in the drawing area to select it and see the handles appear – click and drag any handle to adjust the size. Right-click on a selected object to open the context menu where the appearance of the object can be modified. The screenshot below shows a number of vector objects in OpenOffice Draw – many have been modified to illustrate some of the possible fills.

The range of vector objects include bezier curves, arrows, lines, and also connectors that allow you to quickly create flow charts.

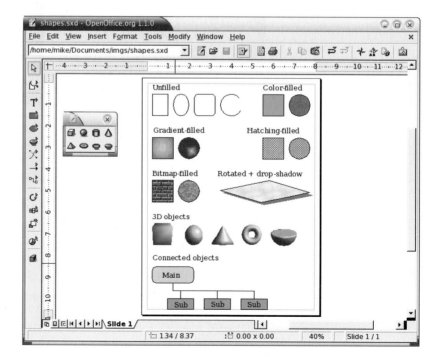

Click the "pie chart" button on the main toolbar to add a default bar chart to the drawing area – all buttons on that toolbar are then replaced by special chart-editing buttons. Place your mouse over each button in turn to reveal the tooltip describing its purpose. You can change the default chart to a different type of chart or graph by clicking the Edit Chart Type button, then selecting one of the options shown in the Chart Type dialog that appears.

Other chart-editing buttons let you adjust the legend, titles, rows, columns, appearance and data values. Click a blank area of the window to exit edit mode and return the standard main toolbar.

To create a chart or graph within a document in OpenOffice Writer use the Insert, Object, Chart menu then click the Create button in the dialog – the default chart is added at the current document location. Double-click this to see the chart-editing buttons – click any blank area of the window to return the main toolbar buttons.

Exported images are rasterized – so they do not contain editable vector objects.

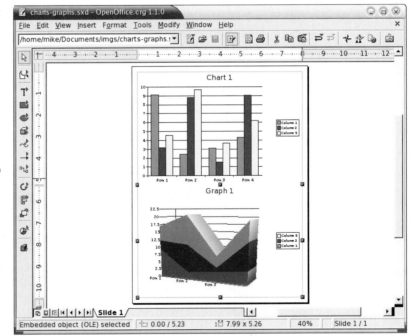

The screenshot above illustrates the default bar chart and its equivalent 3D graph – both main titles have been modified.

charts-graphs.
sxd

To save a drawing click on the File, Save As menu and type a name for the file in the Save As dialog – the native file format for OpenOffice Draw adds the file extension **.sxd**. You can also use File, Export to create a graphic image of the drawing in a wide range of image formats, such as **.bmp**, **.gif**, **.wmf** and more.

Formulas in OpenOffice Math

The Math application within the OpenOffice suite allows mathematical formulas to be inserted into documents in a strictly controlled format. With a document open in OpenOffice Writer click on the Insert, Object, Formula menu to enter formula mode – a "command" area appears at the bottom of the window.

The Math application cannot calculate a formula – it is merely a tool to allow formula formatting within documents.

Right-click on the command area to see the range of predefined formula controls on the context menu. Select any one of these, or type directly in the command area to build the formula. Click in the main window to close the command area and see the formatted formula appear in the document.

In formula mode, click on the Tools, Catalog menu to find a catalog of mathematical symbols that can be inserted into a formula. This includes Greek characters and also has a "Special" collection where you can add your own symbols.

Catalog symbols are referenced by prefixing their name with a `%` character in the command code – in the example shown below `%e`, `%x`,`%B` and `%pi` reference Special catalog symbols. Notice that expressions are enclosed within curly brackets, while the ` tick character and the ~ tilde character add spacing.

OpenOffice does not provide any equivalent to the Access database program found in MS Office – Linux has the more powerful MySQL and PostgreSQL database applications already.

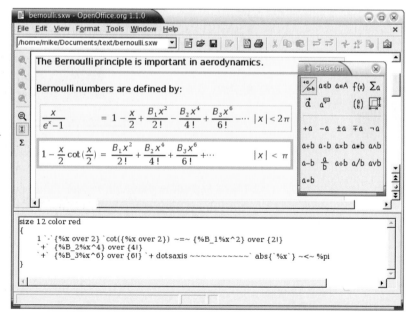

Creating graphics

The most popular graphics manipulation software in Linux is the GNU Image Manipulation Program (GIMP) that is bundled with nearly all distributions. This chapter examines some of the GIMP's prominent features and contrasts the application to the market-leading Adobe Photoshop program.

Covers

Introducing the GIMP | 122

Starting a new image | 124

Finding the menus | 125

Opening selection dialogs | 126

Working with layers | 128

Selecting areas | 130

Using filters | 132

Running scripts | 134

Writing your own GIMP scripts | 136

Chapter Nine

Introducing the GIMP

The GIMP has much of the functionality found in Photoshop. In some areas it even has more capacity – but in other areas it has less. Unlike Photoshop, the GIMP is open-source software available free of charge under terms of the General Public License (GPL).

The results of GIMP plug-ins can be less predictable than those in Photoshop for inexperienced users.

There are over 220 plug-ins included in the standard GIMP installation that cover virtually all the capabilities of the plug-ins that can be purchased as accessories for Photoshop. Many of the GIMP plug-ins are more configurable than those in Photoshop too, which means they can create more powerful effects in the hands of an experienced user.

The GIMP can read image files in the Photoshop **.psd** file format – so if you have a library of files in that format you can use the GIMP to edit them.

One major advantage of the GIMP over Photoshop is its scripting ability – in no less than four scripting languages. For instance, you can write scripts to create custom effects using PERL (Practical Extraction and Reporting Language) scripting – the preferred language of CGI scripts. The scripting capability of the GIMP is unmatched by Photoshop.

...cont'd

The major pitfall of the GIMP is its lack of support for CMYK colors or spot colors, such as PANTONE – it only supports 8-bit RGB, grayscale and indexed images. The GIMP cannot, therefore, compete with Photoshop in the prepress field, but does offer some exciting possibilities in the creation of digital images for the web.

The GIMP is not suitable to produce images for printed material that require CMYK color separation.

When the GIMP is launched for the first time it installs some configuration files – just click OK to accept the default selections. The splash screen (opposite) displays while the application loads.

You will notice that the GIMP looks very different to Photoshop. It opens with The GIMP toolbox dialog, and usually further dialogs for Tool Options, Layers, Channels & Paths, and Brush Selection – like those illustrated below.

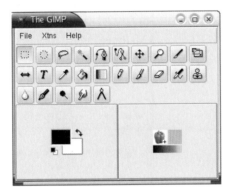

The icons on the buttons broadly correspond to those in the Photoshop toolbox – place the pointer over each icon to see a tooltip appear describing that button's purpose. Notice that The GIMP tools dialog also has menus.

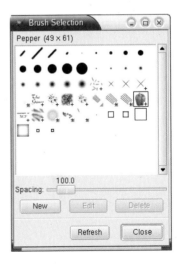

Starting a new image

The initial appearance of the GIMP generally leads new users to question where the menus and working area are – you can only see the File and Xtns menus in The GIMP toolbox dialog, and these contain very little.

The GIMP does not support CMYK color separation.

To access the full GIMP menus a new, or existing, image must first be opened. Select File, Open and browse to an existing image file, or click File, New to create a new image. In the New Image dialog set the Image Size, preferred Fill Type and Image Type – RGB for color or Grayscale for mono. Then click the OK button to open the new image window.

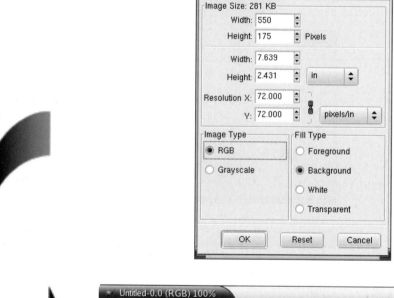

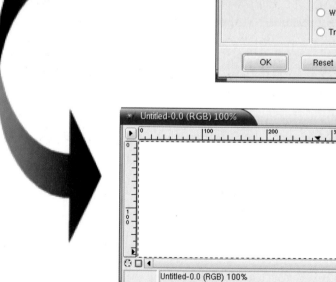

Finding the menus

Right-click on the image window to open the context menu – this contains all the menus and sub-menus that you would normally expect to find on the taskbar in other graphic programs. For instance, to rotate the image through 90 degrees right-click then choose Image, Transforms, Rotate, 90 degrees.

The menus can alternatively be seen by clicking on the arrowed button in the top left corner of the image window.

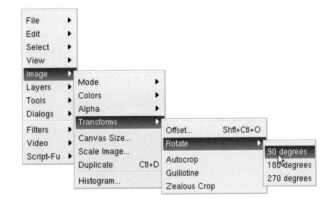

This arrangement initially feels odd if you are used to working in Photoshop but when you get used to it you realize the benefit of moving the mouse much less distance to access the menus.

Select Dialogs, Tool Options on the context menu to open the options dialog for the current tool. Alternatively double-click on any button in The GIMP toolbox to open the options dialog for that tool. For instance, double-click the Pencil tool button in The GIMP toolbox to display the Tool Options for the Pencil tool. These allow you to specify Opacity, Mode and settings for Graphics Tablet input.

The Pencil and Paintbrush tools are very similar but the Pencil will not draw fuzzy edges – even if a fuzzy brush is selected. Shift and click with the Pencil tool to draw straight lines.

Opening selection dialogs

The currently selected foreground and background colors are shown in the bottom left panel in The GIMP toolbox. Double-click on either one of these to open the Color Selection dialog where a new color can be selected.

For instance, double-click on the white background area to open the Color Selection dialog box. Click the approximate color you require in the tall multi-colored panel, then choose a precise color selection in the large colored area – when you click the Close button the chosen color appears in the toolbox panel.

You can also select a color by its RGB, HSV or Hexadecimal value.

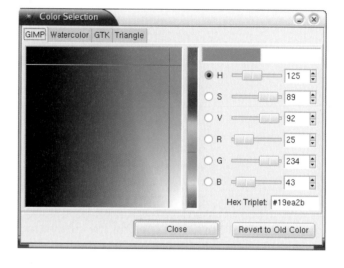

Default colors of black-on-white can be selected by clicking on the small black and white boxes and the selected colors can be switched by clicking the arrowed icon.

The bottom right panel in The GIMP toolbox displays the currently selected Brush, Pattern and Gradient. Click on any one of these to open its Selection dialog – or open them from the toolbox's File, Dialogs menu, or choose the Dialogs option on the right-click context menu.

The Brush Selection dialog contains an interesting range of predefined brushes to experiment with – you can also create your own brush and add it to the available selections.

Similarly, the Gradient and Pattern dialogs contain a range of predefined options to choose from – click on any one to select it. In each case the current selection is displayed in the toolbox panel.

The Gradient tool will apply the current foreground and background colors by default – choose Custom Gradient Blend in its Options dialog to use a selected gradient.

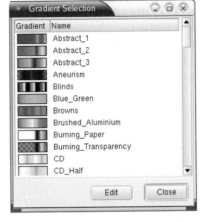

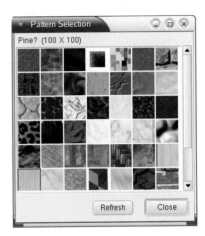

Choose Pattern Fill in the Fill tool's Option dialog to fill with the current pattern.

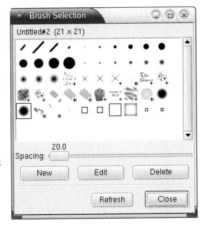

Another useful option under the Dialogs menu allows you to select a Color Palette to work with. The Select tab in this dialog offers a number of predefined palettes to choose from, or you can edit a palette to create your own color range.

If you are creating an image for the Internet choose the "web" palette under the Select tab that contains the 216 colors which are sure to display correctly however they are viewed. Click on the Palette tab to see the available color swatch then choose any of those colors to apply.

Working with layers

The GIMP supports the concept of layers that act like transparent sheets stacked one on the other – the various objects within an image can each be placed on their own layer so they may easily be manipulated independently.

Unlike other graphics software GIMP layers can occupy an area less than the entire image size, unless the objects on that layer fill the whole image. Instead the layers can be optimized to the size of the object on that layer. For instance, a layer containing a text string can simply be the size of that text. This capability saves disk space and improves processing speed.

To create a new layer open the Layers, Channels & Paths dialog under the Dialogs menu, then click on the New Layer button.

The original layer is named "Background" by default – always give new layers a meaningful name so they can be readily identified.

Click the OK button when the New Layer Options dialog appears to accept the default size and settings for the layer – or enter your preferred options first. The New Layer then appears listed in the Layers, Channels & Paths dialog and in the image window. A layer that is smaller than the entire image is surrounded by a dotted line with a yellow background for identification.

To move a single layer hold down the shift key and select the Move tool in the toolbox. Now click on the layer and drag it.

Layers are stacked in order, from the bottom Background layer up, in the Layers, Channels & Paths dialog. Click on a layer to select it then use the arrowed buttons at the bottom of the dialog to change its stack position.

Unlink all linked layers before moving any layer, otherwise all the layers may be moved – even when the linked layers are not selected.

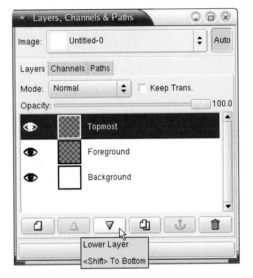

You can click the eye icon of any layer to hide that layer in the image window. Layers can be linked by clicking between the eye icon and the thumbnail box – a cross symbol appears to denote linked layers. Moving a linked layer also moves the layer/s to which it is linked.

Use the Layers, Align Visible Layers option on the context menu to align layers.

A copy of any selected layer can quickly be created by clicking the Duplicate Layer button at the bottom of the dialog box. Drag a layer over the Trash icon then release the mouse button to delete that layer.

To reduce an image with layers to a single layer, with a smaller file size, choose the Layers, Flatten Image option on the context menu. Alternatively, if you wish to preserve the layers save the image in the GIMP's favored **.xcf** file format.

Selecting areas

  The first six tools in The GIMP toolbox are selection tools which provide various ways to select an area of the image for manipulation. The simplest select rectangular and elliptical areas – hold down the Shift key while using these to select perfectly square and circular areas. The Shift key also lets you add further selections and unites them into a single selection if they overlap. Conversely, the Ctrl key subtracts overlapping areas from the first selection. Hold down both Ctrl and Shift to select only the overlapping area.

Once an area has been selected the pointer over the selection changes to cross-arrows that represent the Move tool – you can now drag the selected area to another place in the image.

 The Lasso tool allows for freehand selection of an area of the image. The selected area automatically completes by connecting to its original starting point. You can add to a selection by holding down the Shift key and selecting another area (a + symbol appears alongside the pointer). Similarly you can subtract from a selection by holding down the Ctrl key and selecting another area (a - symbol appears alongside the pointer). Click anywhere on the image window to cancel the selection.

 The Fuzzy Select tool in the GIMP works like the magic wand in Photoshop – click on an initial point and it will select adjacent pixels of similar color until the color becomes too different. Click and drag from the initial point to increase its acceptable range. This tool is ideal for selecting sharp-edged objects within an image.

 The Bezier selection tool in the GIMP works like pen tool paths in Photoshop. Click on the image to choose anchor points around an area you want to select. Finally click on the starting point to complete the selection path. To reposition an anchor point just hold down the Ctrl key then drag it to the desired position.

To create a curve at an anchor point click on the point – two little handles appear. Drag the point so that the handles extend and the selection changes contour around that point. By default the handles are of equal length and create curves with round corners. For greater control hold down the Shift key so you can drag each handle individually to create angled corners. When you are happy with the appearance click inside the curve to complete the selection – the selected area is indicated by a dashed line.

The Intelligent Scissors selection tool in the GIMP is similar to the magnetic lasso tool in Photoshop. Click to select anchor points around a clearly defined object within the image and it will attempt to automatically seek out the edge of that object.

 The anchor points around the large hand in this illustration should be adjusted to more accurately follow the edge of the object.

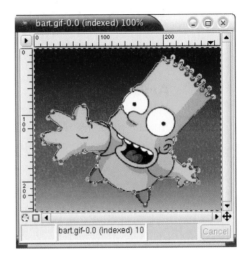

If the line connecting two anchor points does not accurately follow the edge of the object hold down the Ctrl key then click on the line midway between the points. This adds an intermediate anchor point that should correct the problem. Anchor points can be repositioned manually just as with the Bezier selection tool.

When you have surrounded the object click inside the shape to make the selection – the points and lines are then converted to a dashed line indicating the selected area.

Complex selections can be stored in an Alpha Channel so they can easily be recalled later. The selection information regards the selected area as opaque, selection edges as semi-transparent and unselected areas as transparent. To store a selection click inside it then choose Select, Save To Channel from the context menu – it gets added under the Channels tab in the Layers, Channels & Paths dialog. To restore a selection right-click on the Selection Mask Copy on the Channels tab then choose Channel To Selection.

Using filters

Like Photoshop, the GIMP includes a large number of filters that can be used to apply effects to an image. These are accessed by choosing sub-menus of the Filters option on the right-click context menu. The GIMP filters are grouped into the following categories:

Animation

An Animation Player that displays layers as sequential frames and lets you easily create animations in the GIF file format. It also provides optimization to keep those animations compact.

Add a number of different colored rectangles to a white background then use the Artistic, Cubism filter to create an instant masterpiece.

Artistic

Filters to create instant artistic effects, such as cubist paintings and mosaic patterns. These can be applied to the entire image or just to a selected area to add a special effect.

Blur

Many different types of blur filters which are useful to soften part of an image. For instance, to soften a shadow's edge – real shadows seldom have hard sharp edges so it's a good idea to depict them with blurred edges using a suitable blur filter. Additionally, blur filters are useful to disguise skin imperfections and wrinkles in portrait images.

Colors

A range of filters that let you manipulate the Red, Green, Blue (RGB) and Hue, Saturation, Value (HSV) properties of an image or a selected area.

Distorts

Filters that create special surface effects, such as ripples on water, wind effects, waves, whirl and pinch. These filters are especially useful to create textures.

Edge-Detect

Filters that allow you to find the edges of an object as defined by its color boundary. These can be useful to make the selection of an area easy with the Fuzzy Select tool, or to simplify a color fill using the Paint Bucket tool.

Enhance

Useful filters to clean up an image or selection – these let you despeckle, deinterlace and destripe. This category also contains a sharpen filter that is especially useful to make photo images more crisp.

Use Shift+Alt+F keys to bring up the dialog for the last filter you used – use Alt+F to apply the last filter once more.

Generic

Includes mathematical filters that use a Convolution Matrix for image manipulation – this can perform various manipulations but some math knowledge is required to use its possibilities to the full.

Glass Effects

These filters do not create the appearance of various glass surfaces, as you might expect, but rather are useful to create different kinds of lens or curved mirror shapes.

Light Effects

A range of filters that you can use to add shine, lustre and lighting flare to an image or selection. There are a wide variety of lighting effects that can be achieved with these filters but if you are used to Photoshop's excellent Lighting Effects dialog you may find these less intuitive to apply.

Do take the time to read the Tip Of The Day each time you start The GIMP – there are many handy gems in there.

Map

Includes a number of filters that create interesting effects by displacement or distortion relative to an image map.

Noise

Filters that add speckles to an image or selection. These are useful to represent monitor noise or film graininess.

Render

Spectacular effects can be added to images or objects with the filters in this category. These include natural effects, such as clouds and flames, together with pattern effects such as mosaics, grids and jigsaw puzzle.

Running scripts

The GIMP provides support for scripts that can be used to perform a number of set actions on an image. A wide range of custom scripts are included with the GIMP installation – these are written by GIMP enthusiasts and offer some great effects.

Ready-made scripts can be found on the Script-Fu menu located under the Xtns menu in the GIMP toolbox window. There are further scripts available from the Script-Fu option on the right-click context menu in the image window.

Scripts are useful to perform a series of repetitive actions to create an object within an image. For instance, you could create a 3-dimensional sphere object, by filling a circle with an appropriate gradient fill, then create a blurred shadow on a lower layer to give the impression of a ball sitting on a flat surface. The GIMP has a script to execute all the operations needed to create this object very easily – in the toolbox Xtns menu click on the Script-Fu, Misc, Sphere option.

The screenshots on these two pages show the GIMP in a SuSE Linux distro – they illustrate the default style of the SuSE window decorations.

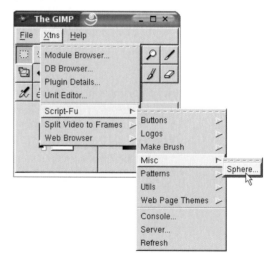

Many scripts initially display a dialog box where you can specify parameters for text, font, size, background and foreground color, and so on. The Sphere script launches a dialog where you can specify the size of the sphere, the direction of the light source, whether to include a shadow, and individual colors for the sphere and the background area.

Press the About key to reveal a description of the script plus details about copyright and the author of that script.

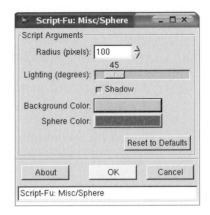

When you are happy with your choices click on the OK button to run the script. In this case the sphere object is created in a new image window – and with the features you specified.

The script items on the context menu are not the same as those under the Xtns sub-menu. Generally, those on the context menu operate on the current existing image window – the others create an object in a new image window.

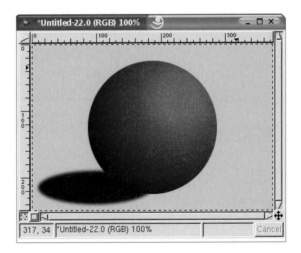

Further free scripts can be downloaded from the Internet and added to the GIMP to provide even more functionality – try searching for "Script-Fu" or visit **www.gimp.org**.

GIMP scripts are typically located in **/usr/share/gimp/x.x/scripts** (where x.x represents the GIMP version number on your system). Copy new scripts to the same directory, then click on the Xtns, Script-Fu, Refresh menu – the new script should now be available from one of the Script-Fu menus in the GIMP.

Writing your own GIMP scripts

Most GIMP scripts are written in the Scheme programming language – these are simply plain text files saved with the **.scm** file extension. If you are interested in creating your own scripts it is useful to first examine existing script files in a text editor. A detailed instruction of scripting in Scheme is outside the remit of this book, but you can find great tutorials at **www.gimp.org**.

To test the execution of Scheme statements click on the Xtns, Script-Fu, Console menu to launch the Script-Fu Console. Type a statement in the Current Command field, at the bottom of the console, then hit the Enter key – the statement is repeated in the Console window along with its resulting output.

Use the DB Browser on the Xtns menu to browse through the alphabetically-ordered GIMP database. Scripts are easy to find as their names usually begin with "script-fu". Existing functions that can be included in your own scripts begin with "gimp-" – the purpose and syntax for each function is given in the DB Browser window.

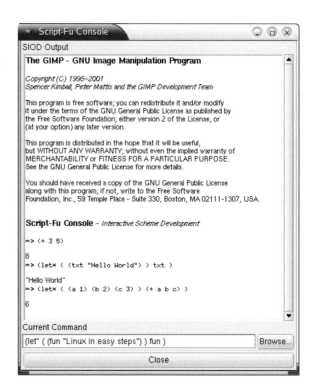

Typically scripts have two parts, the first defines a function that executes a series of operations. For instance, create a content layer, add some content to it, then open a window to display that layer. The second part registers the script with the GIMP to make the script accessible from one of its Script-Fu menus.

Playing sound and video

This chapter demonstrates some of the applications that are bundled with Linux to play various media files for sound, music and video.

Covers

Synthesizing sounds | 138

Playing recorded sounds | 140

Listening to music | 142

Watching videos | 144

Playing and ripping CDs | 146

Burning CDs | 148

Chapter Ten

Synthesizing sounds

One of the most compact file formats for electronic music is that of the Musical Instrument Digital Interface (MIDI). It was introduced back in 1983 through a collaboration between the major electronic instrument manufacturers, including Roland, Yamaha and Korg.

A MIDI file is a text-based set of instructions that can simultaneously control a range of digital devices, such as keyboards, video players, light-show controllers, synthesizers and, of course, computer sound cards.

The encoded instructions in a MIDI file determine the notes to be played together with their position and volume, including crescendos and diminuendos. Other commands specify a numeric reference for each instrument track (0 = grand piano, 74 = flute, etc.) up to a maximum of 16 tracks. They also determine tempo, volume and stereo balance.

The compact size of MIDI files makes them ideal to provide a musical background for web pages – use them sparingly though, as many people just find these irritating.

The MIDI file format has the file extension **.mid**. Files in this format are much smaller than other sound files because they just contain synthesizer instructions rather than recordings of sounds.

In Linux, the major long-standing MIDI application is called "TiMidity" and includes piano and guitar instrument tracks.

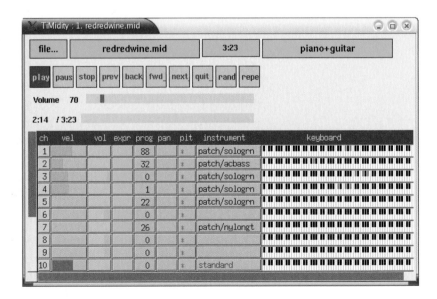

The TiMidity interface harks back to earlier days in Linux but most distros include a modern attractive front-end for this application called KMidi.

Some distros may include the TiMidity++ version – which is MIDI player that can also convert to WAV format.

The illustration above shows KMidi in its extended form with its menus visible – click on the button labelled "KDE Midi Digital Audio" to hide the menus and the bottom panel.

Click on the File menu and browse to a Midi file, then click the Play button to listen to the music. You can choose different options in the KMidi menus to vary several aspects of how the file sounds.

Notice how each track refers to a "patch" – this is a sample of the sound created by each instrument. The patch information is kept in files located in the **/usr/share/apps/kmidi/config** directory. More comprehensive patch sets than the original set are available for download – refer to the KMidi Handbook under the Help menu, or use a search engine, for further information on how to do this.

Playing recorded sounds

Sounds can be recorded in files as digital audio waveform data in the WAV file format. This popular format supports a variety of bit resolutions, sample rates and multiple audio channels.

Another popular format for storing waveform data is the AIFF format, developed by Apple, that is the standard for Macintosh computers. Neither WAV nor AIFF support data compression so, while they record sound data accurately, they can be unwieldy.

"Noatun" is not an acronym – it is simply a name derived from Norse mythology.

In Linux, WAV and AIFF sound files can be played with a KDE application called Noatun – an elaborate front-end for the aRts (Analog Real Time Synthesizer) sound server.

The default interface for Noatun is a simple dialog whose File, Open menu lets you browse to a sound file – click the arrowed Play button to hear the sound.

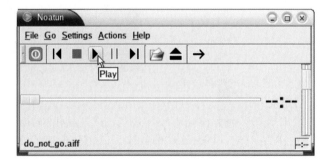

The simple default Noatun interface can be changed to become much more interesting by adding one of the included "skins". Click on the Settings menu then choose the Configure Noatun option to open the Preferences dialog.

Be sure that only one interface option is checked before clicking Apply – or two instances of Noatun will appear.

In the left-hand pane select the Plugins option to display a variety of interface options in the right-hand pane. The default interface "Excellent" will be checked initially. Check an alternative, then click the Apply button, to change the appearance of Noatun.

When the K-Jofol skin has been applied an option "K-Jofol Skins" is added in the left-hand pane. Click this option to reveal the Skin Selector in the right-hand pane – a number of possibilities are available here and further skins can be installed from this dialog.

Extra skins can be downloaded from the web – try KDE-Look.org.

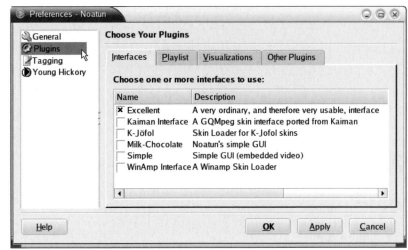

Noatun can handle playlists and is intended to be a multi-media player, in much the same way as Windows Media Player. However, specialized Linux applications have been developed that more ably handle playback of compressed media files for music and video – good examples of these are illustrated over the next few pages.

Listening to music

The WAV format can provide great sound quality but its files are not compact – typically they require 10Mb for each recorded minute. This means that **.wav** files are excellent for short sound clips but unsuitable for pieces of music lasting several minutes.

To address this problem the Moving Picture Experts Group developed the MPEG audio layer 3 format that significantly compresses WAV recordings – an 80Mb file can be reduced to around 5Mb without any noticeable loss in quality. These files have the **.mp3** file extension and are commonly used to store music tracks in a compact manner.

In Linux, the most popular player for MP3 files is the X MultiMedia System (XMMS) application. If you have used the popular WinAmp player on Windows this will look familiar to you.

You can also open the XMMS menu by right-clicking anywhere on its interface.

Click the button in the top-left corner of the interface to open its options menu – here you can browse to a file you want to play or open the Playlist Editor and Graphical Equalizer dialogs.

Use the buttons at the bottom of the Playlist Editor to add or remove tracks to play.

The interface buttons let you play the files and further control options for this are available under the Playback menu.

All three dialog windows can be reduced to occupy minimal desktop space using WindowShade Mode on the Options menu.

WindowShade Mode can also be controlled using the button at the top-right of the interface — the one between the Close and Minimize buttons.

Many other settings may be specified using the Preferences sub-menu on the Options menu. There is also a Skin Browser option that opens the Skin Selector dialog where you can choose one of the many included skins to completely change the appearance of the main interface, equalizer and playlist.

You can install any WinAmp skin for XMMS — just copy it into the directory at /usr/share/xmms/Skins then open the Skin Selector to see it included in the list of skins.

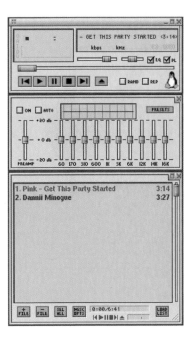

The main XMMS interface constantly scrolls information about the current selection and, when a file is playing, an animation displays the wave peaks and troughs. The appearance of the animation can be widely customized using the options available under the Visualization menu.

Watching videos

The Xine application is a free multi-media player that decodes compressed video files in a wide range of formats including AVI, MOV, MPG, MPEG, ASF, WMV and more.

The Xine (pronounced "ex-een") interface looks like a real DVD player and has three main buttons down the left edge. Click the top button to open the Playlist Editor dialog.

To add videos to the empty playlist click on the Add button to open the MRL browser, then navigate to the location of the video file on your system – use the Select button to add it to the playlist.

You can click the arrowed button at the bottom of the MRL Browser, or the one in the PlayList Editor, to begin playing the selected file.

Add further videos to the playlist as desired then click the Dismiss button to close the MRL Browser dialog. The selected files are now listed in the Playlist Editor dialog – the buttons at the bottom of this dialog let you edit the selection order. When you are happy with the list click the Save button to store your playlist, then click the Dismiss button to close the PlayList Editor. Click on the arrowed Play button in the Xine interface and the items in the playlist are played, sequentially, in a separate window.

Right-click on the video window to hide all other Xine windows – right-click on it again to get them back.

The third button at the left of the Xine interface opens the MRL browser directly – so you can select a file to play instantly, without requiring it to be added to a playlist first.

The Xine interface has the usual media player controls but additionally has buttons to play in Slow Motion and Fast Motion. Also the camera icon button takes a screenshot of the current frame playing and stores in your home directory as a PNG image file.

Click the second button at the left of the Xine interface to adjust video color, brightness and contrast, or to change Xine skins.

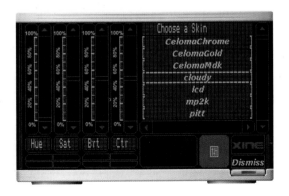

Playing and ripping CDs

The KDE Simple CD (KSCD) application is the standard Linux audio CD player. Its interface has the familiar control buttons that you find on real CD players plus four more for additional features.

Click on the "Compact Disc Digital Audio" logo button to cycle through the displayed time – to show playing time remaining and time elapsed for the track and entire disk. Click the button with the tools icon to open the configuration dialog where you can change the display colors and other simple options. The "i" button helps you search for artist information online, such as concert dates.

The Close button in the top right corner of the KSCD window does not stop the player – select the Quit option from its system tray icon to stop.

The display shows artist and track details if a CD DataBase entry is available – or you can make your own. Click on the button, enter the artist and track details, then click the OK button to save.

If you cannot find the system tray icon you may have accidentally removed the system tray – to recover it right-click on the panel and select Add, Applet, System Tray.

"Grip" is another standard CD application in Linux that can be used to play CD tracks and can also copy tracks to your hard drive in compressed form – converted to the MP3 format. Tooltips appear when you place the point over each button to describe their purpose – click on the "Toggle track display" button to open the tabbed windows.

Click in the Rip column to select individual tracks or click the Rip header to select all tracks.

Audio CDs store music in uncompressed form, as a series of ones and zeros, that Grip can initially copy to the hard drive as a WAV file. It then creates a compressed version in MP3 format and deletes the large WAV file.

Click the Help tab for more detailed information on ripping audio tracks with Grip.

Select the audio tracks that you want to copy ("rip") under the Tracks tab. Then switch to the Config, Encode, Encoder window and set the output format – in the field labelled "Encode file format" ensure that the file extension is **.mp3**.

To copy the selected tracks to your hard drive click on the Rip tab then click the Rip+Encode button – progress bars indicate how each track is copied then encoded in the MP3 format.

On completion, MP3 versions of the tracks you selected can be found in your home directory.

Burning CDs

If your system has a CD writer, audio CDs can easily be created from MP3 files using the KDE K3b application. Launch K3b then click on File, New Audio Project. On the Project menu select the Add Files option to choose the MP3 files you want to put on CD.

Another way to create the Audio Project is to select the MP3 files in the File Manager then, on the context menu, select the option to "Create Audio CD with K3b" – this will launch K3b with the selected files listed ready to burn to CD.

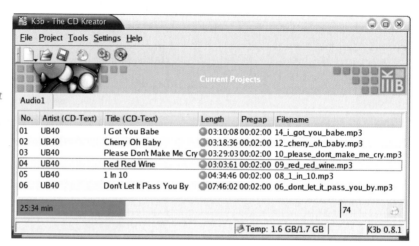

Click and drag the selected files in the K3b window to arrange the order in which the tracks will be written on the audio CD. When you are happy with the order insert a blank CD – then click the Burn option on the Project menu to begin writing the tracks.

The burn process takes quite some time because K3b expands the MP3 files to write them on the CD in the uncompressed format used for audio.

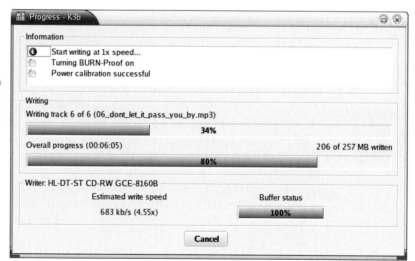

Using the Linux shell

This chapter illustrates how to interact directly with the core of the Linux operating system. It explains the different levels at which Linux can run and how to change between levels. It demonstrates how virtual consoles and shell control are useful when working with multiple shell programs. It also shows how to use a popular shell text editor.

Covers

What is the shell ? | 150

Understanding run levels | 151

Editing with vi | 152

Switching between virtual consoles | 154

Moving between shell applications | 156

Viewing text files | 158

Searching for a word | 159

Printing from the shell | 160

Chapter Eleven

What is the shell ?

At the very heart of the Linux operating system is a core series of machine instructions referred to as the "kernel" – this is a technical program that is not user-friendly, being mainly designed to communicate with electronic components. A Linux shell is a facility that allows the user to communicate directly with the kernel in a human-readable form. It translates command-line instructions, such as those on page 90, so they can be processed.

Most Linux distros include several shell programs that offer different features. The default Linux shell program, however, is the **B**ourne **A**gain **SH**ell (BASH), that is an updated version of the original Bourne shell found in the Unix operating system.

The shell understands a large number of commands and each have a number of optional "flags" that modify their behavior – usually these are prefixed by a hyphen. Many also accept "arguments" that provide data to be used by the command. The typical syntax of a shell command looks like this:

```
command  -flag1  arg1  [  -flag2  arg2  ]
```

Shell commands can be executed from a shell window, such as the KDE Konsole application, on a Linux graphical desktop interface or at a prompt in text interface mode. To confirm the location of the shell program type **echo $SHELL** at a command prompt – it should normally respond with **/bin/bash**.

At a prompt type **who --help** *to see the full list of flags for the* **who** *command.*

You can discover information about users on the system by typing the command **who** at a shell prompt. Using flags with this command can provide other system information. For instance, type **who -b** to reveal the time when the system was last booted.

The Linux boot process calls a command named **init** to start background services for the system environment. The range of services running at any given time is determined by the "run level" – run levels are numbered 0 through 6.

Linux installations that boot straight into a graphical desktop interface will be running at run level 5. Those running in text interface mode will be at run level 3.

To confirm the current run level type **who -r** at a shell prompt.

Understanding run levels

The purpose of each run level is described in the table below.

The root user can see which services are set to run at each level using the command `chkconfig --list` *at a root shell prompt.*

Run level	Description
0	**Halt** – at this level the system is in the process of shutting down
1	**Single-user** – little more than a single console with almost all other services disabled. Typically used for maintenance, such as recovery from hack attacks or repair of disk corruption
2	**Basic multi-user** – most services are running at this level, except for those services that enable network connections
3	**Full multi-user** – starts enabled services in text interface mode but does not start the X Window Server to run Graphical User Interface desktops
4	**User defined** – has no conventional definition but may be custom-configured by the user
5	**Full multi-user graphical desktop** – starts all enabled services including the X Window Server to run Graphical User Interface desktops. Typically this is the default level for most Linux single-user installations
6	**Reboot** – at this run level the system is in the process of rebooting

Typically, the graphical X Window System server can be started from a text interface with the command **startx**, *and can be stopped by pressing the Ctrl+Alt+backspace keys.*

The root user can switch between run levels using the **init** command followed by the run level number. For instance, to change to text interface mode from a graphical desktop interface type **su** to change to super-user root status, enter the root password when required, then type **init 3** and hit Return.

Conversely, to change to a graphical interface from text interface mode type **su** to change to super-user root status, enter the root password when required, then type **init 5** and hit Return.

Editing with vi

The classic Linux shell program for creating and editing text files is the compact **vi** application that is also found on Unix systems – type **vi** at a prompt, then hit Return, to open the text editor.

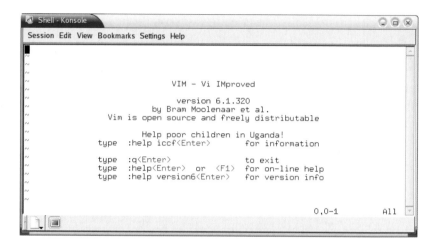

The **vi** editor displays a tilde character at the beginning of each empty line. You cannot enter any text initially as **vi** opens in "command mode" where it will attempt to interpret anything you type as an instruction. Press the **i** key to change to "insert mode" where text can be input – **vi** displays **--INSERT--** at the bottom left corner to let you know it will now accept text input.

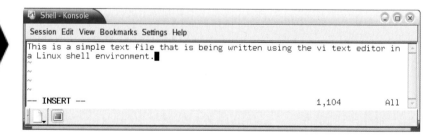

Type some text into the **vi** editor and notice that there is no automatic word wrap at line ends – **vi** will wrap to the next line mid-word unless you hit the Return key to manually wrap to the next line after the last complete word on a line.

There are a number of special key combinations listed in the **vi**

Unlike word processors, text editors have no formatting capabilities.

man pages that let you navigate to different locations in the text but most recent Linux distros use the enhanced **vim** version that let you use the arrow keys on your keyboard for this purpose.

When you have completed text input and want to save it as a file hit the Esc key to exit "insert mode", and return to "command mode".

Type a : colon to begin a command – a colon character appears at the bottom left corner of the **vi** editor. Now type a lowercase **w** (for "write") followed by a space and a chosen name for the text file. Hit the Return key to write the file in your home directory.

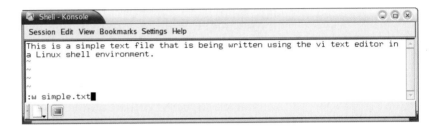

Type **:q** then hit Return to close **vi** and return to a shell prompt.

You can launch **vi** and open a file for editing in one single action – by typing **vi** at a prompt, followed by a space, then the file name.

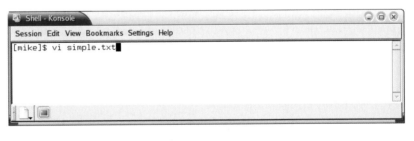

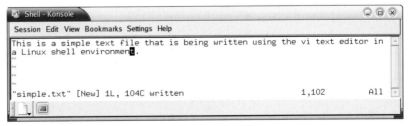

Switching between virtual consoles

Unix, from which Linux is derived, was introduced long before graphical interfaces became popular. It was a text-based operating system that used only a keyboard for input and displayed output on a simple monitor. The term "console" describes the combination of one input device (keyboard) and one output device (monitor).

Linux supports the notion of "virtual consoles" that let you have several full-screen shell sessions active simultaneously. You can easily switch between these using special key combinations. This is useful when you're working with multiple shell programs.

Most Linux installations provide seven virtual consoles by default although you normally only see the seventh – this is the one on which the X Window System is running the graphical desktop. The virtual consoles numbered 1 through 6 do not support graphics. They are, instead, configured to let you execute commands and to run shell programs.

To log out of a console type **exit** *then hit the Return key.*

To open a specific virtual console from the graphical desktop hold down the Ctrl +Alt keys with one hand and press one of the keys F1 through F6 with your other hand – F1 will open virtual console number 1, F2 will open virtual console number 2, and so on. Enter your user name and password to login to the console. To return to the graphical desktop from a virtual console press F7 while holding down the Ctrl+Alt keys.

Use the **who** command to discover which of the six text-based virtual consoles are being used. In the screenshot below the regular user is logged into consoles number 1, 2 and 3 – each console can be running different shell applications, or different instances of the same application.

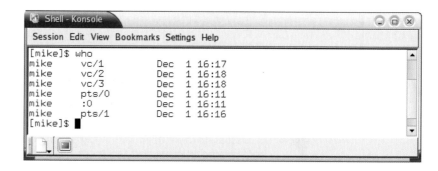

Press Ctrl+Alt+F1 to open console number 1 where, for instance, the **vi** editor could be running.

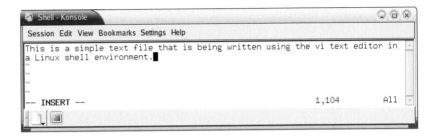

Press Ctrl+Alt+F2 to open console number 2 where, for instance, the user may have the **vi man** pages open for reference.

*You can also get help on vi by typing **info vi** at a shell prompt.*

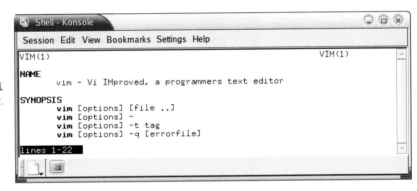

Press Ctrl+Alt+F3 to open console number 3 where, for instance, the user might have the Lynx text-only web browser running to search for information on the Internet.

The Lynx browser is included in most Linux distros but may not have been installed by default – see page 174 for more on installing packages.

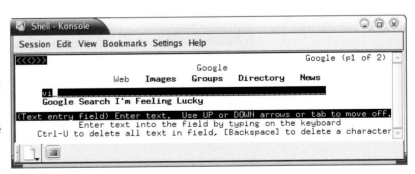

Moving between shell applications

Switching between multiple shell applications running in several virtual consoles can be confusing because it's easy to forget which application is running in each console. Often, a better alternative is to use shell control to suspend and resume running applications.

A running application can be suspended as a "job" by pressing the Ctrl+Z keys. The shell responds with a job number, a "Stopped" confirmation message, the name of the application, and the name of the file it has open where appropriate.

In the example illustrated below, the vi application is first opened to edit an existing file, then the job is suspended by pressing Ctrl+Z. Next the vi info pages are opened, then suspended. Finally the text-only Lynx web browser is opened, then suspended.

Remember that each job gets suspended by pressing the Ctrl + Z keys.

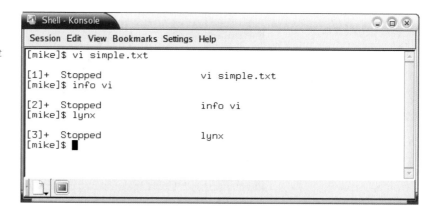

Suspended jobs can remain suspended indefinitely without any problem. Type **jobs** at a shell prompt to see a list of jobs, marking those which are currently suspended as "Stopped".

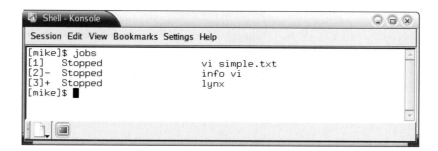

To resume a suspended job type the **fg** (foreground) command at a shell prompt, followed by a space. Add the designated job number, prefixed by a **%** character, then hit the Return key to resume. For instance, the command **fg %1** would resume job number 1 – in this case **vi** would reopen to edit the **simple.txt** file.

Notice how the job resumes with **vi** *in Insert Mode – just as when suspended.*

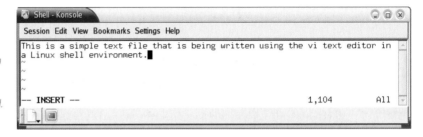

Jobs that take a while to execute can be run as background jobs using the **bg** command to specify their job number. In the screenshot below the **find** command is making a list of all files anywhere on the system that have a **.txt** file extension. It is first stopped using the Ctrl+Z keys, then made a background process so the user can continue to use other shell programs while it runs.

The **-fprint** *flag writes the name of each .txt file on a separate line in a new file, called "txtlist", that it creates in the user's home directory. Notice how background jobs are marked as "Running" in the jobs list until they complete.*

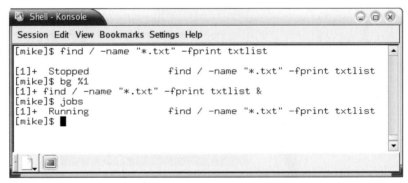

Any job can be terminated using the **kill** command to specify its job number. For instance, the command **kill %3** would terminate job number 3 – and mark it as "Terminated" in the jobs list. When a background job completes it is marked as "Done" in the jobs list. The next time the jobs are listed those previously marked as "Terminated" or "Done" are no longer included.

Viewing text files

To read a text file at a Linux shell prompt navigate to the file's host directory then type the **less** command, followed by a space, then the file name. If the text content is too long to fit in the window the **less** shell program automatically paginates the file.

Use the Space key, or the Page Down key, to view the next page of text content. Use the B key, or the Page Up key, to view the previous page of text content.

The curiously named **less** *program is an enhanced version of an earlier shell program – called* **more**.

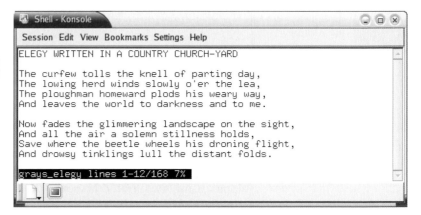

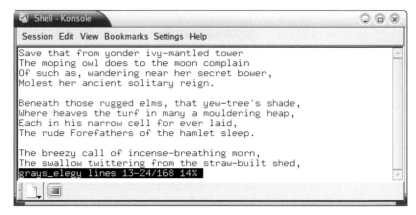

To move down one line use the Down arrow key, or press the Return key. To move up one line use the Up arrow key, or press the K key. Use the Q key to return to a shell prompt.

When viewing a text file with the **less** program you can use the H key for help on a summary of its wide range of commands.

Searching for a word

You can perform a case-sensitive search forward for an individual word while viewing a text file with the **less** program. Type a **/** slash followed by the required word then hit the Return key – all forward instances of that word will be highlighted. For instance, type **/Epitaph** to seek instances of the word "Epitaph".

less *may report that the pattern was not found when attempting to search backwards from the end of text.*

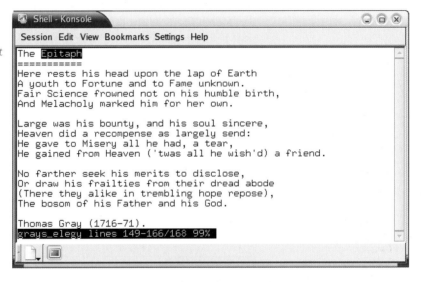

The **grep** shell program offers a powerful alternative way to search text files for a particular word or phrase, and has this syntax:

Sophisticated search patterns can be specified as regular expressions – see **grep man** *pages for details.*

grep *pattern* *file-name*

Again the search is case-sensitive and the **grep** program returns the contents of the entire line where it finds a match to the specified pattern. The **man** page for **grep** lists its many options – **--color** highlights the matched pattern in the returned lines.

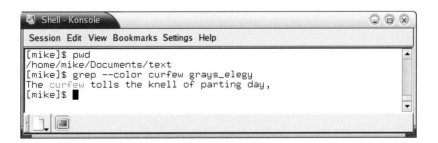

Printing from the shell

To send a file to the printer for printing type the command **lpr**, followed by a space, then the name or path of the file. For instance, to print a file named **simple.txt**, located in your home directory, just type **lpr simple.txt** then hit the Return key to print.

This command creates a print "job" containing the data from the specified file. Each job is placed in a queue awaiting transmission to the printer – when the job reaches the front of the queue it gets sent to the printer and is printed out.

You can examine jobs in the print queue with the **lpq** command – each job is automatically assigned a job number. A job can be removed from the queue, before it gets sent to the printer, using the **lprm** command together with its job number.

In the screenshot below the user initially commands three files to be printed. When the queue is examined the first file has already printed, the second is currently printing, and the third is awaiting transmission to the printer. The user dequeues the third file so it does not get printed out.

A print job can only be dequeued by its owner, or the root user.

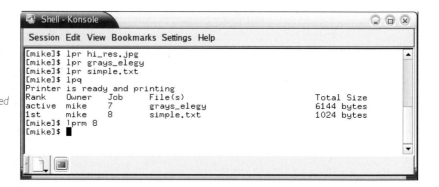

Printing from a shell command prompt is not restricted to simply printing files – data can also be queued for printing using the **lpr** command together with the | pipe character. For instance, you can print a long listing of the contents of the **/etc** directory by piping the results of an **ls** command to the **lpr** command like this:

```
ls -l /etc | lpr
```

Scripting for the shell

This chapter introduces shell scripts that effectively allow you to create your own shell commands. It demonstrates how to write scripts and where to place them so they can be executed from any shell prompt. Examples illustrate how to branch and loop scripts, and how to handle user input.

Covers

Using shell commands | 162

Editing text streams | 164

Substituting variables | 165

Creating a shell script | 166

Branching a script | 168

Looping a script | 170

Handling input values | 172

Chapter Twelve

Using shell commands

Shell scripts allow a number of specified shell commands to be executed in sequence by simply typing the script name at a shell prompt – effectively making the script name a custom command.

Before starting out with scripting it's useful to explore, at a prompt, some of the commands most often used in shell scripts.

The **echo** command can be found in nearly all shell scripts because it writes output information. It takes a string of text as its argument, enclosed within a pair of double quotes. For instance, type **echo "Hello World"** at a shell prompt, then hit the Return key. The shell writes out the text string and, by default, adds an invisible newline character to move the print head to the next line – where a new prompt appears. If the newline feature is not desirable you can use the **-n** option to prevent its inclusion, so the command becomes **echo -n "Hello World"**.

Another useful option for the **echo** command is the **-e** option that allows you to specify simple formatting using "escape" sequences. These all begin with a \ backslash character. The most frequently used escape sequences are **\n** (add a newline) and **\t** (add a tab) – both are used in the screenshot below demonstrating the **echo** command and its options.

Notice that the escape sequences are included within the double quotes – not outside them.

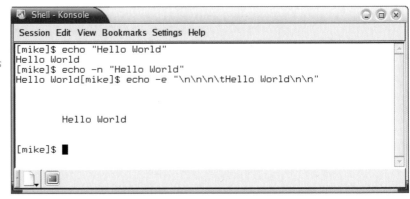

The **clear** command can be used at any time to remove previous content – leaving the cursor at a crisp new prompt at the top of the shell display.

The **expr** command provides the ability to evaluate arithmetic expressions at a shell prompt. It uses the usual operators to add **+**, subtract **-**, divide **/**, multiply *****, and modulus **%** but it only recognizes integer values – it does not work with floating-point numbers.

Attempting to evaluate an expression that contain floating-point numbers will cause an error.

Each value is supplied as a separate argument to the **expr** command so they must have a space before and after. Parentheses can be used to clarify the meaning of the expression, by specifying the order in which it should be evaluated – the arithmetic is performed within the parentheses first, then outside later.

In comparisons the **expr** command returns **1** where the expression is found to be true, or zero if the expression is found to be false. It supports the usual operators to test expressions for equality **==**, inequality **!=**, greater-than **>** and less-than **<** values.

To avoid an interpreter error it is important to surround each multiplication ***** asterisk character, greater-than **>** character, less-than **<** character, and parenthesis character, with quotes.

The results of evaluating some expressions with the **expr** command can be seen in the screenshot below – see how the result of the multiplication example changes after parentheses are added.

*The **expr** command can also be used for boolean arithmetic and pattern matching – see the **expr** man pages for details.*

```
Shell - Konsole
Session  Edit  View  Bookmarks  Settings  Help
[mike]$ expr 21 + 7
28
[mike]$ expr 21 / 7
3
[mike]$ expr 5 "*" 6 - 3
27
[mike]$ expr 5 "*" "(" 6 - 3 ")"
15
[mike]$ expr 25 % 7
4
[mike]$ expr 8 == 8
1
[mike]$ expr 8 != 8
0
[mike]$ expr 9 ">" 4
1
[mike]$ expr 9 "<" 4
0
[mike]$
```

Editing text streams

It is sometimes useful to dynamically edit streams of text to format the output with the shell stream editor **sed**. This is a very powerful and popular application in the Unix/Linux world. It has many options to edit text streams in a variety of ways. The most common one is the **s** (substitute) option that allows a specified string to be replaced by another using this syntax:

sed "s/*seek***/***replace***/g"**

Do not put spaces in the seek and replace parts of the syntax unless they are actually part of the string you want to seek or replace.

The string to replace is represented by *seek* and the new string is represented by *replace*. The final **g** (global) is optional and denotes that all instances of the sought string should be replaced – omitting this will only replace the first occurrence of the string.

In the example below the **more** command first displays the actual file content then **sed** is used to replace the American spelling of the word "color" with its British equivalent. The command makes two substitutions in the output to account for case differences.

*The text in the file remains unchanged – **sed** formats the output stream.*

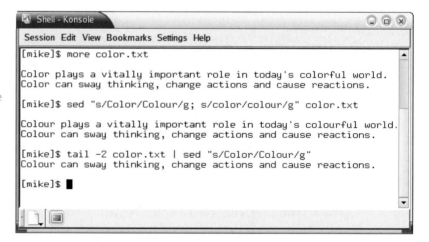

```
[mike]$ more color.txt

Color plays a vitally important role in today's colorful world.
Color can sway thinking, change actions and cause reactions.

[mike]$ sed "s/Color/Colour/g; s/color/colour/g" color.txt

Colour plays a vitally important role in today's colourful world.
Colour can sway thinking, change actions and cause reactions.

[mike]$ tail -2 color.txt | sed "s/Color/Colour/g"
Colour can sway thinking, change actions and cause reactions.

[mike]$ ■
```

*There is also a **head** command that works like the **tail** command – but selects a specified number of lines from the start of the text.*

The final command in the screenshot sends input to **sed** through a pipe using the **tail** command. This selects the specified number of lines from the end of the file. In this case it's the last two lines that are sent to **sed,** which then makes the substitution, and finally displays the output – the last line in this file only contains an invisible newline character.

Substituting variables

A variable is a named "container" in which text and numeric values can be stored. Those values can then be referenced using that variable's name, prefixed by a **$** character – traditionally Linux shell variable names are uppercase.

Values are assigned to a variable using the **=** operator and strings of text should be enclosed in quotes.

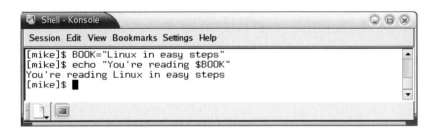

*Type **set** at a shell prompt then hit Return to see a list of all environment variables and their values – you can use the **set** command to assign new values to them.*

Variables remain in existence until the shell session in which they were created is terminated. There are also special environment variables which are constantly available to the shell.

The **$USER** environment variable is useful because it contains the name of the current user and can be useful in scripts to create personalized output without knowing the user's name. The **$PATH** environment variable is also useful as it contains a list of directories that the shell automatically recognizes – when you type a command the shell looks in these for a program by that name.

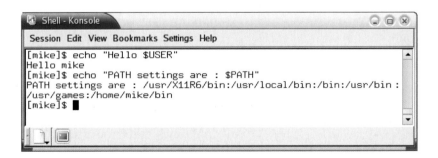

Notice the last directory listed in the **$PATH** environment variable is the **/bin** sub-directory of the user's home directory – this is where shell script files should be placed.

Creating a shell script

A shell script is a plain text file containing a series of commands that allow repetitive sequences to be performed whenever the script is executed – by entering its name at a shell prompt. This is like creating a new custom command of the script name.

The script can simply comprise a single command, or a list of commands – exactly how they would be typed at a shell prompt. For instance, the color of the font in a shell window can be set by the **echo** command, with its **-e** option to allow escape sequences to be interpreted, and the desired color stated using its American National Standards Institute (ANSI) code reference.

The example below demonstrates how the font "brush" can be changed through different colors from a prompt.

The colors represented by the ANSI codes can vary.

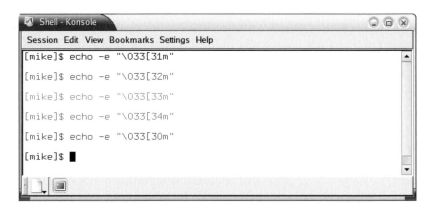

These commands are not very user-friendly so you may prefer to create a script to change brush colors if you want to do this often.

To create a new script open any plain text editor, such as vi, then type the following code at the beginning of the first line:

```
#!/bin/bash
```

This is sometimes called the "sh-bang" line, after the **#!** characters – whenever Linux reads these at the beginning of a file it looks in the specified path location for an interpreter to execute the script. In this case it is the bash shell program, that is located in Linux's **/bin** directory.

Comments can be added to a shell script using the **#** character – any characters following this on a line are ignored. It is useful to add comments below the sh-bang line to describe the purpose of the script, author, date of creation, and so on.

Now type the command, exactly as you would at a shell prompt, then save the file in the **/bin** sub-directory of your home directory. Set the script file's permissions, to make it executable, then type the file name at a shell prompt and hit Return to run the script.

The "red-brush" script shown below is saved at **~/bin/red-brush**. It changes the shell font color to red and displays a formatted message whenever it's executed.

The ~ character is shorthand for your home directory – such as /home/mike.

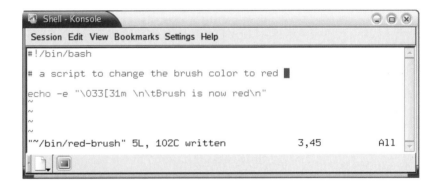

Use the 700 permission to make a file read, write and executable for the user only.

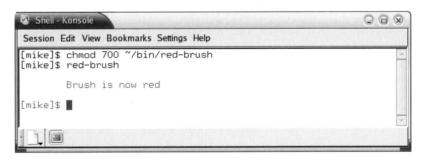

Similar scripts could be created for each available color – blue-brush, black-brush, green-brush, and so on – but it would be better to encapsulate these choices within a single script. The example on the next page builds upon this initial script by adding "conditional branching" to apply the desired color according to an input option.

Branching a script

It is often desirable to have a shell script implement a specific action according to the condition of a tested value. For instance, when testing a boolean value, a script could execute a certain action when the tested value has a true condition and a different action when it has a false condition.

An **if-then** statement is the simplest way to test a value to determine if an action should be implemented, with this syntax:

```
if[test-expression];then action fi
```

The action will only be implemented when the tested expression is true – when it's false the script simply moves on. Notice that an **if-then** statement must be terminated with the **fi** keyword. Multiple commands can be included in the action part of the statement for execution when the tested value is true.

if-then statements can be nested to form complex blocks – but each one must end with the **fi** keyword.

You can provide an alternative action to be executed when the tested value is false by adding an **else** keyword to an **if-then** statement, like this:

```
if[test-expression];then action else action fi
```

This statement is suitable when testing a value which may have only two conditions but for those values which may be more varied it is necessary make repeated tests using the **elif** keyword – a combination of **else** and **if**:

```
if    [test-expression];then action-1
elif [test-expression];then action-2
elif [test-expression];then action-3
fi
```

Typically a value input by a user will be stored within a script variable. This value can then be evaluated as a test expression in an **if-then** statement to allow the script to execute specific actions according to the result of the test – a procedure referred to as "conditional branching". For instance, the following script presents a menu of font brush colors requesting the user to select a integer value for their preference. The user input is assigned to a variable named **CHOICE** by the **read** command. This variable value is then tested in an **if-then** statement, and an appropriate command is executed according to the result of the evaluation.

This script is saved as a file at ~/bin/brush, given executable permissions, then called by typing **brush** *at a shell prompt.*

It is important to preserve the spaces as they appear in this script – adding or removing spaces can render the script erroneous.

```
Shell - Konsole
Session  Edit  View  Bookmarks  Settings  Help

#!/bin/bash

# a script to change to any brush color

# first clear the screen
clear

# write a menu of color options
echo -e "\033[30mFont Brush Menu - Please select a color:"
echo -e "\033[30mBlack\t[0] "
echo -e "\033[31mRed\t[1] "
echo -e "\033[32mGreen\t[2] "
echo -e "\033[33mBrown\t[3] "
echo -e "\033[34mBlue\t[4] "
echo -e "\033[35mPurple\t[5] "
echo -e "\033[36mCyan\t[6] "
echo -e "\033[30mExit\t[7]"

# store user input in a variable
read CHOICE

# change color and confirm the choice or quit
if   [ $CHOICE == 0 ]; then echo -e "\033[30m \n\t Brush is Black\n"
elif [ $CHOICE == 1 ]; then echo -e "\033[31m \n\t Brush is Red\n"
elif [ $CHOICE == 2 ]; then echo -e "\033[32m \n\t Brush is Green\n"
elif [ $CHOICE == 3 ]; then echo -e "\033[33m \n\t Brush is Brown\n"
elif [ $CHOICE == 4 ]; then echo -e "\033[34m \n\t Brush is Blue\n"
elif [ $CHOICE == 5 ]; then echo -e "\033[35m \n\t Brush is Purple\n"
elif [ $CHOICE == 6 ]; then echo -e "\033[36m \n\t Brush is Cyan\n"
else exit
fi
~
~
"bin/brush" 31L, 1004C written                    3,41          All
```

```
Shell - Konsole
Session  Edit  View  Bookmarks  Settings  Help

Font Brush Menu - Please select a color:
Black    [0]
Red      [1]
Green    [2]
Brown    [3]
Blue     [4]
Purple   [5]
Cyan     [6]
Exit     [7]
1

         Brush is Red

[mike]$
```

Looping a script

A script can be made to repeatedly execute commands for every item in a list with a **for-in** loop statement. Typically this specifies a variable that references successive items in the list on each iteration of the loop – the first item on the first iteration, the second item on the second iteration, and so on. Its syntax is:

Supply a list of file names to a **for-in** *loop to have the same command actions performed on each file.*

```
for var in item-1 item-2 item-3
do
        action/s
done
```

The more traditional **for** loop, from the C language, can also be used to repeatedly execute commands in a shell script. This typically has a counter variable, traditionally named **i**, that loops until it reaches a specified value. It is assigned an initial value in the **for** statement which also includes the terminal value, as a test expression, and a means to change the counter on each iteration – usually this is incremented on each iteration. This loop's syntax is:

```
for(( initializer; test-expression; change ))
do
        action/s
done
```

Both type of **for** loops feature in the example script shown below.

The **++** *increment operator increases the current value by one (***i++*** is short for* **i=i+1***). Similarly, the* **--** *decrement operator reduces the current value by one.*

```
#!/bin/bash

# a script to demonstrate for loops

# a for-in loop
for x in one two three
do
        echo "Number $x"
done

# a C-style for loop
for (( i = 1 ; i <= 3 ; i++ ))
do
        echo "Number $i"
done
~
"loop" 15L, 203C                              5,17        All
```

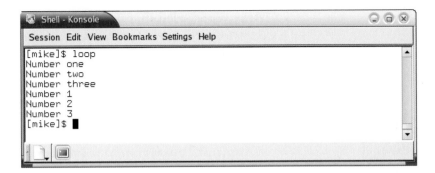

An alternative loop format can be written using the **while** keyword. This typically requires a counter variable to be assigned an initial value which is used in the test expression on the first iteration of the loop. When this is found to be true the loop executes its command actions – these should include a statement to change the value of the counter variable, otherwise an infinite loop may be created.

An infinite loop will never end – but the job can be manually stopped using the Ctrl+Z key combination.

```
#!/bin/bash

# a script to demonstrate a C-style while loop

i=1                              # initialize the counter

while (( i < 4 ))                # test expression
do
        echo "This is line $i"   # write the current count
        (( i++ ))                # increment the counter
done

~
"while-loop" 12L, 232C                          12,0-1      All
```

```
[mike]$ chmod 700 while-loop
[mike]$ while-loop
This is line 1
This is line 2
This is line 3
[mike]$
```

Handling input values

Arguments added after a script name at the prompt are automatically stored in sequentially numbered variables – the first argument can be referenced in the script as **$1**, the second as **$2**, and so on. Longer strings of text, including spaces, can be stored in a script variable using the **read** command.

Output with the **echo** command is, by default, written to "standard output" – which means it is displayed by the monitor. Alternatively output can be redirected to a text file using the **>** character. Further redirections to the same file will overwrite the original text, but additional text can be appended instead using **>>** redirection to add new text after the original text.

The "input" script below stores two argument values, then reads text input by the user. It displays the input and stored values, then writes them to a text file named **input.txt** in the working directory.

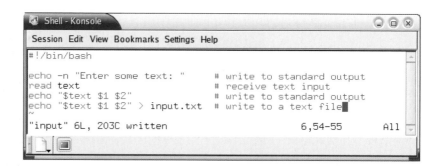

Use the **pwd** *command to discover the current working directory.*

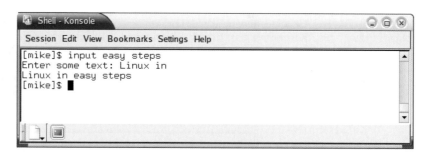

Shell scripting is a powerful feature in Linux and the examples in this chapter serve only as an introduction to some of its many possibilities. Further advice can be found on the Internet – try typing "bash programming" into a search engine.

Extending your Linux system

This chapter illustrates how to install and remove applications on a Linux system – both from the distro CD and via the Internet. It also demonstrates how to install other desktop environments and how to switch to them from the familiar KDE desktop. A number of resources are provided where you can find the latest news about Linux development, together with useful tips and advice.

Covers

Installing packages | 174

Removing packages | 176

Downloading packages | 178

Installing downloads | 180

Installing other desktops | 182

Switching between desktops | 184

Linux resources | 186

Chapter Thirteen

Installing packages

Most Linux distros include the RedHat Package Management (RPM) tool which simplifies installation of additional applications. This is the equivalent of the Add/Remove Programs feature in Windows and is located on a menu in the system Control Center.

In Mandrake Linux the installer is called "RpmDrake". Launch the Mandrake Control Center, click on the Software Management icon in the left pane, then select the RpmDrake Installer icon in the right pane to open the Software Packages Installation dialog.

The options at the top of this dialog help you locate a package by search, or by changing the way in which the available packages are listed.

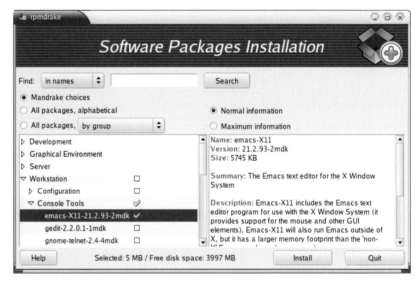

You can select multiple packages from the menus if you want to install several applications at once.

The Software Packages Installation dialog displays a number of expandable menus that let you select an application to be installed. For instance, to add the popular "emacs" text editor to your system (if it is not already installed) expand the Workstation and Console Tools menus, then select the emacs package from the list.

To begin the installation process click on the Install button. If the selected application requires additional support packages to also be installed a dialog will appear requesting your approval – this has a More Infos button where you can discover more about the support package. Click on the OK button to proceed, or click the Cancel button to abort the installation.

For the next stage of the installation a dialog appears requesting you insert the appropriate distro CD containing the application.

Insert the CD then click the OK button – a new dialog appears displaying a progress indicator illustrating the package installation.

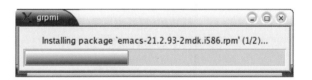

Upon completion a final dialog appears confirming that the installation succeeded.

Launch emacs then select the Tutorial option under its main Help menu to discover more about emacs.

Click on the OK button to finish the installation process. A menu item for the emacs application should have been added to the Start menu under Applications, Editors. Click on this to launch emacs in graphical mode, or type **emacs** at a console prompt to launch it in text mode.

Removing packages

In some Linux distros the package installer that uses the RedHat Package Management (RPM) tool is also an uninstaller that lets you remove packages from your system.

In Mandrake Linux the uninstaller in "RpmDrake" is separate from that used to install packages. Launch the Mandrake Control Center, click on the Software Management icon in the left pane, then select the RpmDrake Uninstaller icon in the right pane to open the Software Packages Removal dialog.

Be careful not to select a group rather than a specific package to avoid removing multiple applications by mistake.

In the Software Packages Removal dialog select the option to display all packages in alphabetical order – these are then listed in the left pane so you can select an application to be removed. For instance, to remove the "emacs" text editor that was installed on the previous page scroll down the list to find that application.

The emacs installation required an additional support package to be installed so there are two "emacs..." entries listed. The top one contains the libraries required to run the text editor – click on this to select it for removal and a dialog box appears informing you that you must also remove the second emacs package.

Click on the More Infos button to read details about what the second package actually does, then click OK to proceed.

Always examine the More Information dialog details to become familiar with the purpose of each package.

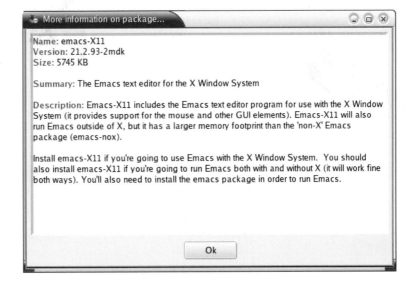

Both emacs packages get checked in the list to indicate that they are selected for removal – click the Remove button to uninstall them.

A small dialog appears while the packages are being removed.

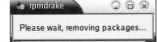

Upon completion the dialog disappears, the emacs application is no longer available, and its entry in the Start menu has been removed.

Downloading packages

In the KDE desktop the Konqueror web browser can be used to easily download RPM packages via File Transfer Protocol (FTP). Start Konqueror then choose the Open Location option on the main Location menu to launch the Open Location dialog. Type the name of an FTP site into its Location field then click the OK button to connect to the specified site. For instance, to download the Opera web browser RPM package via FTP launch the Open Location dialog and type **ftp.opera.com** then click OK.

Konqueror connects to the Opera FTP site and displays the contents of its root directory – a text file containing a welcome message and a sub-directory named **/pub**. Click on this directory icon to reveal its contents and continue to navigate through the file system to find the RPM package you wish to download.

Most FTP sites that offer files for free download accept the word "anonymous" as the login username and your email address as a password – Konqueror supplies these automatically to log you right in.

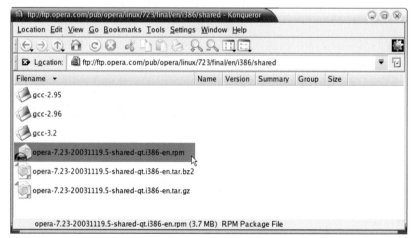

Click on the RPM package and a Question dialog asks whether you want to download or open the file – click the Save As button.

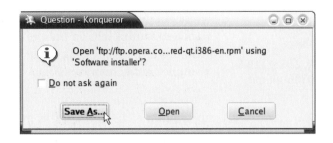

You can also drag'n'drop files from Konqueror onto your desktop.

When the Save As dialog box appears navigate to a destination location for the download package – the Desktop is usually most convenient. Click the Save button to begin the download and a dialog appears displaying a progress indicator.

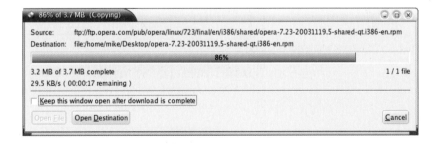

opera-7.23-20031119.5-shared-qt.i386-en.rpm

When the download completes an RPM icon appears at the chosen destination and the package is ready to be installed on your system.

Installing downloads

opera-7.23-20031119.5-
shared-qt.i386-en.rpm

To begin installation of an application from a downloaded RPM package simply click on the package icon. For instance, click on the icon of the Opera RPM package downloaded to the desktop in the example on the previous page.

A message dialog asks you to confirm that you wish to install the application – click on the OK button to proceed.

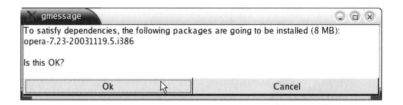

You can discover more about GPG online at http://gnupg.org.

A further dialog may now appear displaying an apparent error message "No GPG signature in package". GPG is an acronym for Gnu Privacy Guard – the Linux equivalent of the PGP public key encryption system that can be used for file verification. The Opera RPM package file, and most other files, do not use GPG so this warning message can be safely ignored. Click the Yes button to proceed with the installation.

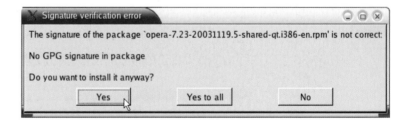

A small dialog appears displaying a progress indicator as the Opera web browser application is being installed on your system.

The RPM package file can be deleted after installation has been completed.

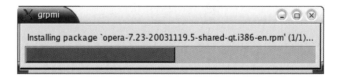

When the installation completes Opera has been installed in the **/usr** directory and a menu item has been created on the Start menu.

You can drag the Opera icon onto the toolbar to create a Quick Launch button.

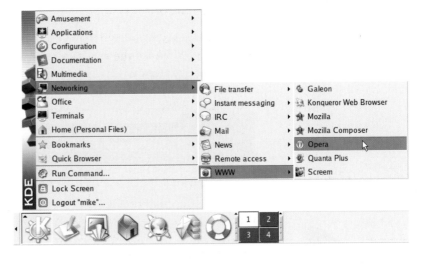

Click on the Opera icon, or type **opera** at a prompt in a shell window, to launch the Opera web browser.

Installing other desktops

The Gnome desktop environment is the popular alternative to the KDE desktop for many Linux users. It can be installed from most distro CD sets in the same way as any application.

In Mandrake Linux, launch RpmDrake then select the Gnome Workstation option under the "Graphical Environment" menu. Click the OK button in the dialog that appears to accept the additional packages which Gnome requires.

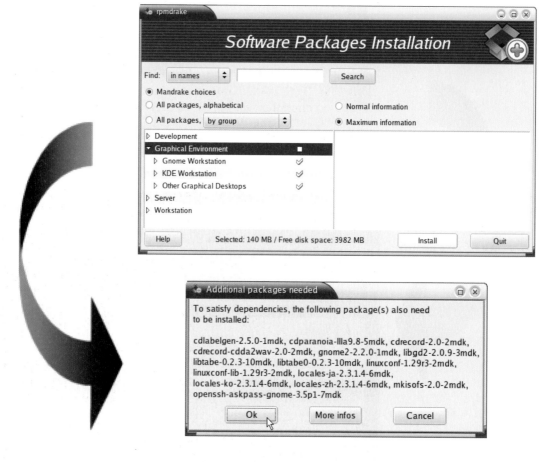

Insert the distro CD when requested, then click on the OK button to begin the installation – another dialog box appears displaying a progress indicator that illustrates the package installation process.

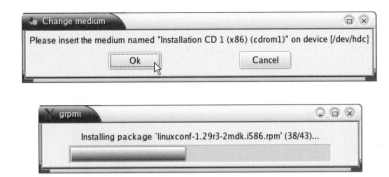

Upon completion a dialog confirms the successful installation of the packages. Open the Mandrake Control Center, click on the Boot menu, then select the DrakBoot option. Change the System Mode options to start Gnome with autologin when the system boots, then click the OK button to apply the update.

Reboot the system and Linux will now automatically login the default user into the Gnome desktop environment.

Discover more about the Gnome project online at www.gnome.org.

Switching between desktops

When you click the Start, Logout menu in a graphical Linux desktop a Logout dialog presents the options to halt or reboot the computer and also offers to login as a different user.

The appearance of the Logout and Login dialog boxes vary according to the display manager in current use – the Logout dialog shown here is from the K Desktop Manager (KDM) and the Login dialog is from the Gnome Desktop Manager (GDM).

Choosing the option to login as a different user closes the current graphical desktop and displays a Login dialog. A Login dialog lets you choose which desktop environment you wish to launch. For instance, in the Gnome Desktop Manager Login dialog select your preferred desktop environment from the Session menu.

The System, Configure menu allows you to change certain aspects of the Login dialog's appearance.

Next enter your user name and password, then click the OK button to start the selected desktop.

Many Login dialogs have a "face browser" of possible users – click on your user icon to enter the user name in the text field, then click OK and enter your password.

If you choose not to login to another desktop the Login dialog can also be used to halt or reboot your Linux system.

Linux resources

The examples in this book hopefully demonstrate that the free Linux operating system, and the open-source applications bundled with most distros, are perfectly capable of performing all the routine daily requirements of most desktop users.

Additionally, those features of Linux that are not available in other operating systems present new exciting possibilities.

Fittingly, for a network operating system, there are abundant resources on the Internet that help you discover more about Linux. The most obvious first call is the website for your chosen distro – for instance, Mandrake Linux users should visit the Mandrake website at **www.mandrakelinux.com**.

The ISO files are large so download requires a high-speed Internet connection.

Disk ISO images of most freely-available Linux distros can be downloaded from **www.linuxiso.org**. These can then be burned to CD-ROM to produce a Linux distro installation set.

A wealth of general Linux information can be found on the Linux Online website at **www.linux.org**. This includes links to lots of Linux application home pages, downloads and documentation.

Help on all Linux matters can be sought from the vast community of Linux users, developers and enthusiasts in the Linux Forum at **www.linuxforum.com**. This site hosts many individual forums on specific Linux topics including troubleshooting hardware and distribution-specific issues.

A weekly review can be found in the Linux Weekly News at http://lwn.net.

You can read about all the latest Linux developments on the Linux Today website at **http://linuxtoday.com**. This excellent site is updated daily with Linux news from around the world.

Lots of interesting articles about Linux appear in the monthly printed publication "Linux Magazine". Worldwide subscription is available online at **www.linux-mag.com**, where you can also read some great feature articles.

These, and many more, online resources let you keep pace with the latest innovations as Linux continues its progress into the desktop operating system market. They can help develop your skills to take full advantage of the power and flexibility that Linux offers – created and backed by the global open-source community.

Index

A

access permissions   102
add (+) operator   163
add/remove programs feature   174
adding a second HD drive   15
adding an application button   50
address book   72
alpha channel   131
American National Standards Institute (ANSI)   166
animation filter   132
archive   106
arithmetic operators (+, -, *, /, %)   163
aRTs sound server   39
assign (=) operator   165
automatic login   35

B

background   56
bash shell program   166
Basic Input Output System (BIOS)   18
bezier selection tool   130
bg (background) command   157
blur filter   132
boot menu   36
boot sequence   18
bootloader   31
Bourne Again SHell (BASH)   150
branching   168
brush selection dialog   123, 126
bunzip2 command   108
burning CDs   148
Bzip2 program   108

C

case-sensitivity   82
cd command   90
CD writer   148
charts   118
chat   80
chkconfig command   151
chmod command   103
chown command   103
click'n'drag action   50, 55
CMYK colors   123
color (script)   167
color palette dialog   127
color scheme   58
color selection dialog   126
colors filter   132
command line   90
command mode (vi editor)   152
compressing files   106
configure panel   51
configuring the mouse   20
connecting to the internet   66
console   154
control center (system)   34
copy action   96
copy'n'paste action   54
cp command   97
CPU speed   12
current command field   136
cut action   96

D

database (DB) browser   136
defragment the HD drive   16
deleting files   98

desktop background   56
desktop theme   60
desktop wallpaper   57
desktops   182
diagrams   118
directory tree   82
disk ISO image   186
disk partitioning   22
display managers   48
distorts filter   132
distributions, distros   10
divide (/) operator   163
do keyword   170
done job   157
done keyword   170
dos and don'ts   92
downloading packages   178
DrakBoot   34, 36
DrakConf   35
DrakConnect   66
DrakFloppy   34
DrakxTV   44
drive letters   82
dual-boot   36

E

echo command   150, 162
  -e option   166
edge-detect filter   132
elif keyword   168
elliptical selection   130
else keyword   168
emacs text editor   174
email client   70
embed objects   110
enhance filter   133
environment variables, $USER, $PATH   165
equality (==) operator   163
escape sequences   162, 166
event sounds   62
execute permission   103
expr command   163
extracting files   106

F

false condition (script branching)   168
fg (foreground) command   157
fi keyword   168
file manager   88
file permission   102
File Transfer Protocol (FTP)   76, 178
filters   132
find command   157
for loop   170
for-in loop   170
FTP program   77

G

Gabber, IM client   80
generic filter   133
get command   77
GIMP   122
  scripts   134
  toolbox   125
glass effects filter   133
Gnome desktop environment   9, 182
GNU   9
  General Public License (GPL)   8, 122
  Gnu Privacy Guard (GPG)   180
gradient dialog   126
graphics tablet input   125
graphs   118
greater-than (>) operator   163
grep command   159
Grip CD application   147
group permission   102
Grub bootloader   36
gunzip command   107
GZip program   107

H

HardDrake   38
hardware suitability   12
HD drive capacity   12
head command   164
help   64
home button   89

I

if-then statement   168
inbox   72
inequality (!=) operator   163
info command   64
init command   150
input   172
input redirection <   172
insert mode   152
installation   18
   summary   32
installing downloads   180
installing packages   174
instant messaging   80
internet connection   66
IP address   67

J

Jabber application   80
JavaScript console   69

K

K Desktop Environment (KDE)   9
   control center   55
   help center   64
   KDE Window Manager (KWM)   62
K3b CD burner   148
KDE Simple CD (KSCD) application   146
KEdit text editor   94
kernel   10
keyboard configuration   48
KeyboardDrake   48
kill command   157
KMidi MIDI player   139
Konqueror   52
   file browser   88
   web browser   68
KSnapshot screen grabber   100

L

lasso tool   130
launching applications   52
layers   128
layers, channels & paths dialog   123, 128
layers, flatten image option   129
less command   158
less-than (<) operator   163
light effects filter   133
LILO bootloader   36
links   101
Linux Forum website   186
Linux Magazine website   186
Linux Online website   186
Linux Today website   186
Linux Weekly News website   186
login, automatic   30
login dialog   184
logout dialog   41, 184
LookNFeel menu   55
loops   170

lpq command 160
lpr command 160
lprm command 160
ls command 77
  -a option 90
  -l option 102

M

magic wand 130
magnetic lasso tool 131
man command 64
Mandrake Control Center 34
Mandrake Linux 11
manual pages 64
map filter 133
master (MA) drive 15
Master Boot Record (MBR) 31
mcc command 35
memory size, RAM 12
messaging 80
Microsoft Office 110
MIDI file format 138
mkdir command 105
modulus (%) operator 163
more command 85
mount command 105
mounted drives 82
mouse configuration 48
MouseDrake 48
Mozilla
  Address Book 72
  Composer 78
  email client 70
  JavaScript console 69
  Messenger 70
  newsgroups 74
  preferences 69
  web browser 68
MP3 file format 142
multiply (*) operator 163
Musical Instrument Digital Interface (MIDI) 138
mv command 97

N

navigating (the file system) 88, 90
Network Interface Card (NIC) 66
new file 94
new image dialog 124
newsgroups 74
Noatun application 140
noise filter 133
NTFS file system 105

O

OLE objects 110
open command 77
OpenOffice 8, 110
  Calc - spreadsheets 110, 114
  Draw - charts, graphs, diagrams 118
  exporting documents for Word 112
  Impress - presentations 110, 116
  Math - formula formatter 110
  Writer - word processor 110 – 111
Opera web browser 178, 180
output redirection >, >> 172
owner (permissions) 102

P

packages 26, 174
panel-hiding buttons 51
PANTONE 123
parentheses 163
partition 14, 22, 24, 82
password manager 71
paste action 96
path 82

pattern dialog   126
PDF file   95, 113
permissions   102
Photoshop   122
pipe | 160
playing music   142
playing sound   140
plug-ins   122
popup windows, suppression   69
Portable Document Format (PDF)   95, 113
presentation   116
printer configuration   42
PrinterDrake   42
printing   160
pwd command   91

Q

quick-launch button   50

R

read command   168
read permission   103
rectangular selection   130
Redhat Package Management (RPM)   174, 176
redirection >, >>, <   172
refresh menu   135
removing packages   176
render filter   133
reposition taskbar   50
resources   186
RGB color   124
ripping CDs   146
rm command   99
rmdir command   99
root directory, /   82
root password   28
root user   82
run command   52
run level   150

S

ScanDisk   16
scanner configuration   46
ScannerDrake   46
Scheme programming language   136
screen resolution   40
screensaver   61
Script-Fu   134
    console   136
scripts   134
security level   21
selecting areas   130
selection dialogs   126
sh-bang line   166
shell   150
shell application   156
shell commands   162
shell font colors   167
shell window   53
shortcuts   100
slave (SL) drive   15
slide show   116
sound card configuration   38
sphere script   134
spreadsheet   114
standard output   172
start button   50
start menu   51
startx command   35, 151
stream editor, sed   164
su command   151
sub-directories   83
substitute (text)   164
subtract (-) operator   163
super-user   82, 88
suppressing popups   69
SuSE Linux   134
suspended job   156
switching between desktops   184
symbolic links   101
synthesized sound   138

T

tail command   164
tar program   107
   cf, tf, xf, z options   107
tarball   106
taskbar   50
terminated job   157
text file   158
theme   60
themes, Mozilla   68
tool options   123
toolbox   123
transferring files   76
trash   98
true condition (script branching)   168
TV card configuration   44

W

wallpaper   57
WAV file format   140
web browser   68
web page editor   78
What You See Is What You Get (WYSIWYG)   78
while loop   171
who command   150, 154
window appearance   58
window color   58
window decorations   59
window style   59
Windows partition   104
winmodems   13
write permission   103

U

uninstalling   176
UNIX manual pages   64
user account   29

X

x window system   154
XFdrake   48
Xine video player   144
XMMS MP3 player   142
XSane program   46

V

variables   165, 172
vi text editor   152
video   144
view buttons   88
virtual console   154
virtual desktops   54

Z

zoom buttons   88